Ethical Dilemmas in
Social Work Practice

Margaret L. Rhodes

Ethical Dilemmas in Social Work Practice

ROUTLEDGE
NEW YORK AND LONDON

First published in 1986
by Routledge & Kegan Paul plc

Reprinted in 1989 by
Routledge, an imprint of
Routledge, Chapman and Hall, Inc.
29 West 35 Street
New York, N.Y. 10001

Published in Great Britain by
Routledge
11 New Fetter Lane
London, EC4P 4EE

Library of Congress Cataloging in Publication Data

Rhodes, Margaret L.

Ethical dilemmas in social work practice.
Bibliography: p.
1. Social workers, Professional ethics for.
2. Social case work. I. Title.
HV10.5.R49   1986   174'.9362   85–14504

ISBN 0-7102-0366-7
ISBN 0-415-90157-X (pbk)

British Library CIP data also available

For my parents
Elizabeth Fleming Rhodes
Kenneth Olney Rhodes

And in memory of my maternal grandmother:
Margaret Eaton Brown Fleming

Contents

Acknowledgments

In writing this book, I am indebted first and foremost to my students – at Simmons College, the University of Redlands, and most of all the College of Public and Community Service, University of Massachusetts, Boston. They have encouraged me, asked the tough questions and showed me the importance this kind of book might have.

Many others have helped directly or indirectly, and I only regret that I will not be able to mention all of them. From my early days of doing social work, I am indebted to Elise Cayer Bernstein and John Moore for their insights into the profession. Alasdair MacIntyre, my teacher, has profoundly influenced the way I think about philosophy, and although he probably does not know it, he gave me the courage to write what I wanted. Particularly in the early stages of the book, the support and suggestions of Judy Levine, Carol Baker and the Randolph Cooperative Mental Health Component/South Shore Mental Health Center were invaluable.

Many others have read drafts or offered other kinds of help. I am particularly grateful to Larry Blum, John Arras, Vicky Steinitz, and Betty Reid Mandell for their detailed comments on the manuscript. I would also like to thank Harriet Rosenstein, Owen Flanagan, Gene Sapadin, Elizabeth Fleming Rhodes, Ted Rhodes, Howard Cohen, Brad Honoroff, Jeremy Brecker, Linda Tsang, Elaine Werby, and John Strange for their help. For their unfailing encouragement to me while I was writing, I owe immense gratitude to Stephanie Rhoades, Sabra Price, Ann Helwege, Herbert Krohn, Lucy Horwitz, Margo Boetticher, Sandra Kanter and Clark Taylor. I thank Louis Palena for his support over many years, especially during the last stages of this project. Kelly Gerry and Ellen Prydekker provided both typing and advice. Joyce Walworth offered valuable editorial assistance in the last, difficult stage of writing. I am also grateful to my editor, Stratford Caldecott, for his assistance.

I owe a special and deep thanks to Louise Dierker, who enabled me to think about my work and life in new ways.

Finally, my profoundest gratitude goes to three friends whose support is inseparable from the writing of the book.

Since we were graduate students at Brandeis together, Carol Ochs has encouraged my love of, and doubts about, philosophy. Our dialogue has persisted for twenty years; it has shaped my view of philosophy and has been a great joy. When I have been ready to give up, both in doing philosophy and in writing this book, Carol has often kept me going.

Without Ann Withorn, the book would not have been written. She urged me to write it and made suggestions about every chapter. Our discussions have been one of the greatest pleasures of doing the book and have informed the writing in more ways than I can say.

Finally, Jennifer Radden has offered suggestions on every aspect of the book. Through the week-by-week writing and editing, she has always been there, offering ideas and bringing new energy. Our discussions about social work ethics, mental illness, philosophy, and numerous other topics have been a constant delight and have reaffirmed my belief in the value of doing philosophy together.

In this book, I argue for the importance of dialogue, and dialogue has given the book its life. Its shortcomings and misconceptions are entirely my own.

Margaret L. Rhodes
Boston, February 1985

Overview

When I first studied philosophy, ethics was presented as an august, esoteric subject far removed from the concerns of daily life. My professors taught me to ask such questions as "if there is a good, how can we be sure it is?" or "Does knowing do any good?" If students foolishly ventured to ask about the meaning of life or about how to act *today*, they were regarded with bemused condescension and sent over to the humanities or sociology department. I left philosophy after two years of graduate study and plunged into social work. For three years as a caseworker in a public child welfare agency, I found myself confronted daily with the most difficult ethical issues I had ever encountered. Nothing in the training for the job and nothing in my graduate work prepared me for handling these issues. Later, when I completed part of a Master's degree in social work, I found that there, too, nothing addressed the ethical issues social workers regularly confront.

Eventually I returned to graduate work in philosophy, completed my degree, and began teaching. My interest has centered on bridging the gap between the heights of philosophical speculation and the daily, messy, concrete ethical problems faced by human service workers.

My experiences in both worlds serve as the inspiration for this book. My students at the College of Public and Community Service, University of Massachusetts, Boston, have provided a continuing source of material and have convinced me that this sort of applied ethics can enrich the social work field. Day after day, social workers face complex and perplexing ethical issues that cry out for analysis and understanding, yet neither social work texts (which primarily focus on social policy or clinical techniques) nor philosophical texts (which focus on theoretical issues) address these issues.

I begin each chapter where social workers begin their day – with the client – an individual or family with whom a social worker has some relationship. The social worker must decide how to act, given demands made by the client, agency, profession, colleagues, and society.

An *ethical dilemma* is usually defined as a choice in which any alternative results in an undesirable action. When, for example, we have promised confidentiality to a client, who tells us something that endangers others, we have an ethical dilemma. If we uphold the confidence, we may contribute to harming others. If we violate the confidence, we violate our trust. Whatever we do, we seem to be "in the wrong." Many social work situations pose dilemmas of this sort.

Even more important, social workers face ethical dilemmas which are obscure and thus often unrecognized. Without awareness of the subtle but pervasive dilemmas in human services, workers run the risk of having their ethical ideals gradually eroded without even realizing how or when this erosion took place.

My purpose in this book is three-fold: (1) to show how our actions as social workers always emerge from ethical and political assumptions, whether or not we recognize them; (2) to examine how the ethical stands required of us (by profession or agency) imply consequences which may be inconsistent with our goals; and (3) to explore how we can use ethical analysis to make our work more consistent with our goals.

The cases described in this book are composites or fabrications. No case-study corresponds to any actual case, although many will seem familiar because they are so typical of social work practice. The book is not systematic in the sense of attempting to cover all important issues. Instead, some central ethical issues are explored in depth, in the hope that the *process* of analysis will then be applied to other issues.

Throughout the book, I refer to the social worker as "she," even though there are many male social workers. The usage of "he/she" would be awkward and tiresome, and to use the standard "he" inappropriate, given that the profession is predominantly made up of women.

Each chapter centers on a case-study that typifies a central problem in social work practice. We shall see how decisions about particular cases reflect complex combinations of psychological, ethical, and political assumptions. I focus on a few prominent and conflicting ethical perspectives, which are reflected in case decisions. Through this book, I want to encourage recognition of these basic conflicts and invite serious dialogue about them. Only through debate about our real differences can we arrive at informed ethical stands to guide our practice.

Chapter 1 focuses on the wide variety of ethical and political assumptions implicit in any case decision. The social work Code of Ethics is examined, as are recent attempts to provide an ethical basis for social work practice.

Chapter 2 sketches some of the ethical perspectives that so confusingly permeate our decisions. It also outlines the ethical perspective adopted in this book.

In *Chapter 3*, the issue of confidentiality is explored: a worker's responsibility to maintain client confidences versus responsibilities to society or the agency.

Chapters 4 and 5 consider how workers influence and should influence clients: in what ways do our values affect treatment? When is manipulation coercion? When is coercion justified?

Chapter 6 focuses on problems in bureaucracies: should one disobey agency directives when they go against client interests? What should a worker do about incompetent supervisors or co-workers? How does one balance responsibility to the agency with that to society, clients, and oneself?

In *Chapter 7*, we return to workers' responsibility to clients, in order to explore more fully the professional altruistic relationship.

Finally, *Chapter 8* offers some suggestions for enlarging the dialogue to which this book contributes.

1 Facing dilemmas

> The Mind becomes accustomed to things by the habitual sight of them, and neither wonders nor inquires about the reasons for the things it sees all the time.[1]

A case-study: ethical issues

> Mrs Joanne Smith, twenty-three years old, brought her one-year-old son, John, to the hospital at 5 on a Thursday afternoon, because John had severe burns on his arms. The attending doctor also found bruises and abrasions on his legs and buttocks and marks on his back that looked suspiciously like cigarette burns. The mother appeared agitated and eager to leave the hospital. When asked how the burns occurred, she replied that she had no idea; she was in the bedroom and the children were watching television when it happened. John had somehow overturned some water that was heating on the stove.
>
> The doctor filed a petition of suspected child abuse, as legally required, and referred the case both to the hospital's social service unit and to the child abuse unit of the appropriate agency. Mrs Smith, informed of these actions, then returned home with John.

Child abuse units are mandated to investigate such cases and to do whatever necessary to protect the child. The assigned social worker received some additional information from the hospital, whose social worker had seen Mrs Smith on Thursday afternoon:

> She described Mrs Smith as an attractive woman – blonde, shoulder-length hair, 5 feet tall, very thin – who herself had bruises on her legs and face. She was neatly dressed in a light blue suit, and her breath smelled of alcohol. John was dressed in his pajamas. Answering questions reluctantly, Mrs Smith repeated several times that she did not need help. She lived in a two-bedroom apartment of a public housing project with her two other children (ages four and six) and her boyfriend, Tom, the father of John. Tom worked in the

post office and she sporadically as a waitress at a nearby restaurant. When she worked, John stayed with her mother, who lived a few miles away. The two older children were in school.

This case may seem extreme, but in many ways it is typical of social work practice. Social work as a profession commits itself to helping the desperate, even the "untreatable."[2] Despite the wide range of activities from private practice to prison counseling and community action, social workers most frequently do casework in an agency setting (mental health clinic, hospital, public welfare agency) where such cases are common: the unmanaged and unmanageable aspects of social life, like child abuse, wife battering, poverty, retardation.[3] Social workers confront a bewildering array of legal, medical, educational, social and economic issues, and since they concern themselves (at least in theory) with the individual's general welfare, they do not have the luxury of focusing solely on a legal or medical problem.

Cases like this one contribute to the sense that understanding ethical issues in some rational, systematic way is simply impossible. The immediate decisions seemingly leave no time or energy to sit back and consider abstract, "idealistic" ethical claims. A decision must be made quickly; a child's life may be in danger.

We may thus be tempted to gloss over ethical decisions as obvious or technical. We know that the highest priority is the child's life. If that life is in danger (a factual matter), the worker should remove him from the home and find the best available placement, a technical matter, based on evaluation of the family's strengths, the child's needs, and resources. These seemingly technical matters regularly receive the most attention – in supervision, in case presentations, in social work education and, I believe, in social workers' thinking.[4]

The ethical choices, however, surround us. Consider the case again. Before we can usefully analyze the social worker's choices, we have to consider how she should even begin to think about it.

She faces major conflicting obligations simply in deciding who the client is. She is to provide service to the parents and the child, and yet their interests may differ. In addition, they may all have different views about what is in the *child's* best interests. What if, for example, the grandmother wants to take John, while the mother wants him to be at home and the father wants to place him in a foster home? Who should decide, and on what basis? Should the social worker even inform the grandmother of the situation if the mother does not wish it?

Even if we can decide whose welfare is primary, assuring the client's welfare may conflict with maintaining his or her rights. What are John's rights or the mother's? The mother has the right to refuse all help and to take the case to court (where she might win). Should the social worker encourage her to consider this option seriously? If the worker allows John to remain in the home only on condition that the mother receive help, is that coercion without due process?

Whatever the social worker does commits her to fundamental ethical claims. For the purposes of analysis, we can distinguish ethical assumptions which are then reflected in our social/legal, personal, professional and skill-based responsibilities.

Fundamental assumptions

At the most fundamental level, the social worker's decisions reflect philosophical assumptions about the nature of help and of our obligations to others.

HELPING THE CLIENT:

(1) Helping: is it desirable?
(2) What counts as "real help"?
Who is the client?
What is in the client's best interest?
What sort of social structure is consistent without our goals?
(3) Who should decide?

(1) Casework theory assumes that we ought to help others – that casework itself is good. The sort of helping involved in casework, however, may not be good or may even be harmful. We must consider that possibility.[5] (2) When we help clients, we also make assumptions about what counts as help and what is good for a particular client. But we can only make sense of

our help (our goals for the client) in a broader context of the sorts of persons, relationships, and society we are trying to promote: society as it is now structured, some idealized form of that structure, or an alternative one. Does the good of some individuals or groups count more than that of others? Why? What do our answers reveal about our view of society? (3) Finally, we make assumptions about who should decide any of these issues. Are the client's interests those that the client articulates, the society recognizes, the agency advocates, the social worker decides, or some combination thereof?[6]

In the case of Joanne and John Smith, we can see fundamental ethical claims most clearly in assumptions about family. "Family" has become a controversial topic: we disagree about whether it is desirable, how it ought to function (if at all), or even what it is.[7] Our decisions about John will involve judgments on these issues. Is the grandmother considered part of the family? How much authority should Joanne and Tom have over their children, and how should they exercise that authority? What are the rights of children and parents? In much of the psychiatric and social work literature on the family, the ethical assumptions are implicit, with focus on techniques of family intervention.[8]

Social/legal assumptions

The social worker must carry out the policy of her agency. If the agency's goals conflict with her clients' interests, she must decide what to do. To illustrate with a common sort of problem: because of financial constraints the agency may discourage providing day-care or other services that would enable John to remain at home, even if that is a better solution than placing him in a foster home. To avoid foster placement, the worker has to violate the rules of her agency. What ought she to do? What assumptions does she make?

Other conflicts arise from our obligations to society. The social worker may be subpoened by the court for her records if, for example, Joanne Smith becomes involved in a custody battle with her former husband for the children. If the social worker turns over the records, she will be violating confidentiality and jeopardizing the trust of her client. What ought she to do?

Personal assumptions

Until now, I have said nothing of the social worker's own values. They may conflict with those of the client, agency, other colleagues, profession, or society. The social worker is required to act "impartially" as a professional, but also to act on the values of the agency and society. What if society passes legislation which the social worker believes to be immoral? Perhaps a law is passed requiring that parents on Aid to Dependent Children work, and the social worker believes this would result in increased neglect of Joanne's children. Should she help Joanne to disobey the law?

The social worker's values may also conflict with those of her client. She cannot or should not always put aside her own beliefs. Even apart from clear-cut wrong-doing by the client, value differences pose problems. Suppose, for example, that the social worker seeing Joanne Smith has a strong belief against abortion and discovers Joanne is pregnant and considering abortion. The social worker's quandary is this: if she says nothing about her belief, then she feels she will be betraying herself and may influence Joanne Smith anyway in subtle ways without intending to. If she shares her point of view, will she then influence Joanne unduly? What should she do?

Consider a somewhat different situation. Suppose that Joanne Smith is a deeply religious Catholic and the social worker an atheist who believes that religion is at best a silly and ineffectual crutch. Won't her beliefs inevitably have some impact on how she views the case? Should she request that Joanne Smith see a different worker, whose views are closer to her own? Does Joanne Smith have a right to know the social worker's views?

Radical differences in values raise questions for us about the influence a social worker should have over a client. Particularly if the treatment plan includes establishing a relationship of trust and exploring the client's beliefs, we must ask whether a client has a right to know something about the beliefs of the worker. The social work literature discusses this question only around a few controversial topics, where the worker's values clearly harm clients – sexism, racism, or cultural bias – but discussion has remained limited to those issues.

Skill-based and professional assumptions

Most broadly, social workers develop an expertise that is intended to help clients but may create an elitism that serves to alienate workers and clients from each other. Joanne Smith may well interpret the worker's presence as one more person pushing her around. Further, workers learn professional goals that are inherently conflicting. In the Smith case, for example, the worker must both investigate and offer help to the family – be an inspector and an advocate, as well as promote her own career.

Besides her broad, professional judgments, a worker makes many seemingly narrow and technical choices. Before making a decision about the Smith family, the social worker must learn more about the family and the resources available to them and thus must have skills of interviewing, case-recording, psychological evaluation. At least some of these choices seem relatively free of ethical judgments.

Again, appearances are deceptive. Ethical assumptions enter into these so-called technical matters in a number of ways. Take, for example, interviewing techniques. We can only evaluate an interview if we know what its purpose is: we must know what we want to find out about a client or what we think a client should notice or think about. The social worker will ask Joanne Smith some questions and not others, and her questions will reveal her values. The choice to interview Joanne instead of the whole family itself reflects ethical assumptions about who is most in need of help.

While these ethical considerations may seem unproblematical, often they are not. Certainly, in our broad choices of technique we make ethical choices: behavior modification, drug treatment, psychotherapy. Suppose, for example, that John is a hyperactive child, who cannot be controlled by his mother. His behavior can be efficiently and inexpensively controlled with drugs, but the long-range effects are unknown and the drug may make John sleepy most of the time. Should John take the drug? Should the social worker make a strong recommendation or leave it entirely up to the parents? On what basis should she decide?

Even narrow technical matters can pose problems in ways

that reveal ethical assumptions. The social worker, for example, may present the Smith case at a staff meeting. What are the Smiths' rights to confidentiality? How much ought the social worker to reveal? What if the family does not want anyone except the social worker to know parts of their family histories? What are their rights to information from the presentation? What if they want to attend? My point is not that they should necessarily be able to enforce their views here, but that the social worker's seemingly technical decision commits her to assumptions about clients' rights, the nature of professional relationships, and the limits of power over others' lives.

To give another example, one of the social worker's goals may be to get the younger children into a day-case center, seemingly another technical matter. Its ethical components only become obvious in a crisis. What if, for example, the mother insists that no information about battering be revealed to the day-care personnel? How should the social worker weigh the mother's right to confidentiality against the day-care center's right to information? What if the mother is strongly in favor of using a day-care center that offers educational enrichment but only custodial care?

The underlying assumptions in these decisions should not remain, as they have, an unquestioned part of "professional standards." Even when the assumptions are challenged, for example if Joanne Smith should object to a case presentation, there is a tendency to dismiss or discredit the challenge (Joanne Smith is acting-out) and not to use it to examine seriously the underlying ethical issues.[9] The underlying issues only emerge in a crisis, at which point we do not have time to think about them.

The chart below outlines the key ethical questions which we shall answer, directly or indirectly, in making casework decisions:

CASEWORK

A GOALS What are the goals? What are the worker's responsibilities?

(1) to the client – who is the client?
– what is the client's good?

(2) to society – what sort of society?
(3) to the agency – what values does the agency embody?
(4) to the profession – what ethical assumptions do professional commitments incorporate?
– what assumptions do professional techniques include?
(5) to oneself – what is essential to one's integrity?

B DECISION-MAKING PROCESS: Who should decide the goals and responsibilities (client, worker, agency, community, profession, government)?

Until now I have been using a mixed and undefined ethical vocabulary – referring indiscriminately to rights, obligations, responsibilities, goods, oughts, interests, ethics, values. I have done so because that is in fact the way that everyone, except perhaps philosophers, talks about ethical issues. I do not mean at this point to presuppose any particular ethical system by the use of any of these terms. My point is that social work decisions involve fundamental ethical commitments and the choices often pose conflicts among them.

There are other ethical issues which the Smith case might present. The issues mentioned, however, are more than enough to make social work ethics look even more hopeless than before. We started with a single case and from it generated many interrelated ethical problems, including the nature of individual welfare and the welfare of society. To respond to all of these issues would seemingly paralyze the social worker; it would be months before she could make any decision about John's placement. In addition, the ethical and political issues seem large and remote from the immediate needs of this family. Perhaps the social worker would do better simply not to think about them, after all. She should just get on with the business of helping people as best she can. As one of my students put it: "You can't ever get any final answers. It's frustrating; I'd rather study something where you can know you're right."

Resolving ethical issues is not, however, a hopeless undertaking. First, we need to distinguish two kinds of ethical problems: (1) those which are resolvable; and (2) those which demand action but are not resolvable. In our ordinary lives, we make this distinction all the time: if, for example, your child has an incompetent teacher who is excessively punitive, you can usually do something about it. You write the mayor, organize others in the neighborhood, etc. If, however, your child has a fatal disease, you cannot solve the problem. You must do what you can to ease the child's suffering, perhaps to prolong the child's life, but you cannot "solve the problem."

In social work, because there are political and social pressures to believe that all social problems are resolvable, we can easily forget this distinction. The social worker takes on problems no one has been able to solve (alcoholism, prison conditions, poverty), as well as the pain and suffering that are a natural and unavoidable part of life (old age, disabilities, death). As social workers, we must recognize the immensity of the task we are expected to do and the inevitable failures that must result.

Second, only recently have social workers begun seriously to analyze ethical issues in the profession. Only in the past twenty years have social workers (as a group) designed ethical guidelines.[10] These attempts have been limited by the sharp boundaries among professions, with the result that social work for the most part has not been enriched by work done in fields such as philosophy. The situation is now beginning to change, and one can imagine the emergence of new approaches to social work ethics and of increased debate. Having time to consider ethical issues, or rather making the time, will reduce feelings of hopelessness and helplessness.

Finally, we cannot escape these ethical questions. We must focus on them if we want to act well towards others and act with personal integrity. As professionals, we have power over clients' lives and our moral choices can radically affect them, for good or ill. If we avoid the issues, we run the risk of acting in muddled or damaging ways, blindly assuming that we are "helping others" when we may not be.

Further, our ethical stands may be gradually eroded by little changes in agency policy and in our practice, without our realizing it. Faced with a difficult moral choice, we may be totally unprepared to handle it. For example, suppose you discover that a co-worker is incompetent and the situation requires immediate action. If you have not thought much about these issues, then you are more apt to feel overwhelmed and to act in ways you later regret.

We begin with a case-study because it illustrates three themes that will be developed in this and subsequent chapters. (1) Almost every decision that a social worker makes, even a technical one, is a decision about ethics. (2) It is also a decision about politics, and this usually makes social workers uneasy. Our case decisions make assumptions about what sort of society and governmental regulations we deem desirable. (3) Particular cases reveal the full complexity of social work choices. Cases should thus be the starting point of our ethical and political deliberations and the final test of the viability of proposed guidelines.

Given the complexity of social work decisions, we could benefit from systematic guidelines for resolving ethical issues. The social work Code of Ethics attempts to provide just such guidelines, to which we shall now turn.

N.A.S.W. Code of Ethics

The Code of Ethics published by the National Association of Social Workers (N.A.S.W.) gives the ethical standards (both general principles and specific rules) that professional social workers are expected to follow.[11] In its own words, "This code is intended to serve as a guide to the everyday conduct of members of the social work profession and as a basis for the adjudication of issues in ethics . . ." (iii). It "is based on the fundamental values of the social work profession . . ." (iii). The code goes on to elaborate the way in which it is to serve as a guide to everyday conduct.

> In itself, this code does not represent a set of rules that will prescribe all the behaviors of social workers in all the complexities of professional life. Rather, it offers general principles to guide conduct . . . in situations that have ethical implications. It provides the basis for making judgments about ethical actions before and after they occur. Frequently the particular situation determines the ethical principles that apply and the manner of their application. In such cases, not only the particular ethical principles are

taken into immediate consideration, but also the entire code and its spirit. (iii)

The standards set forth in the code put in even starker relief the conflicts that emerged in the case of Joanne and John Smith. The code is divided into six major areas of the social worker's responsibilities. The first includes standards of personal conduct and of professional competence. The other five consist of responsibilities to client, colleagues, employers, the social work profession and society.

While these responsibilities are spelled out in some detail, their conflicting claims are not explained. The social worker's fundamental obligation is to the client whom she is to serve with loyalty, devotion, determination and competence (II.F.1). She is also told, however, to promote the welfare of society (VI.P.). What if a client's interests conflict with the good to society? Suppose that the client is running an illegal business or is shoplifting or is selling heroin to children? Is the worker's responsibility in these situations to the client or to society? Does it depend on the seriousness of the danger? Can anything more be said about the importance of these responsibilities with respect to each other?

The social worker will also have conflicting responsibilities to the client and colleagues, to colleagues and society, and so on. In fact, the case-study revealed precisely this sort of conflict. While the code thus gives social workers a list of ethical principles, those principles as they stand are of little help in resolving most of the difficult ethical choices that social workers confront.

Any ethical code will generate controversy about how it applies to particular cases and how its principles should be interpreted. And in many ethical systems the principles (or virtues or goods) lack any clear ordering. Think about the Ten Commandments in the Bible, for example. Two of the commandments tell us to honor our parents and not to kill. Killing in self-defense is a problematical case; should it count as killing or not? Is going to war a case of self-defense? Even if we accept the commandment, we are sometimes unsure how to apply it. Further, if killing is necessary to honor your father who orders it, which commandment should take precedence?

Although this sort of conflict is not always resolvable, the Ten Commandments serve as guidelines for conduct within the context of belief in a certain sort of God who has a particular relationship to a group of people. The Commandments are justified in terms of that God and that relationship. The broader context can be used to help resolve conflicts between principles. The social work Code of Ethics is, however, significantly different in its structure, because it is a set of principles without any clear underlying justification or framework.

The absence of any explicit ethical or political framework comes out most clearly in what is said about the social worker's responsibilities to society. "The social worker should promote the general welfare of society" (VI.P.). This responsibility is broken down into seven parts:

(1) The social worker should act to prevent and eliminate discrimination against any person on the basis of race, color, sex, age, etc.
(2) The social worker should act to ensure that all persons have access to resources and services they require.
(3) The social worker should act to expand choice and opportunity for all persons.
(4) The social worker should promote conditions that encourage respect for diversity of cultures.
(5) The social worker should provide appropriate professional services in public emergencies.
(6) The social worker should advocate changes in policy and legislation to improve social conditions and to promote social justice.
(7) The social worker should encourage informed participation by the public in shaping social policies and institutions.

The first three parts and the sixth concern fairness and justice. The social worker is to act so as to bring about services, opportunities, and expanded choices for all persons, particularly those who are disadvantaged or discriminated against. More generally, the social worker "should advocate changes in policy and legislation to improve social conditions and to promote social justice" (VI.P.6).

The responsibility to promote social justice and a better

society, however, only have content if we are told what makes for social justice and general welfare – what sort of society, what concept of justice, what sort of governmental regulations, what relationships among people. Only in this broader context can we know what will benefit the client, who would be part of that welfare, or our colleagues or profession.

In our society today, there is no general agreement on these fundamental concepts. The "new right's" conception of justice, for example, differs from the "liberals'" which differs from "socialist" conceptions. These differences are important because only by spelling out the nature of justice can the social worker know what responsibility she has "to promote social justice" and "to improve social conditions" (VI.P.6). For example, arguments are made for and against welfare benefits on the grounds of social justice. What position ought the social worker to take? Clearly, her position will affect the legislation she promotes (VI.P.6) and what she advocates for her clients (II.F.1). It will also affect how the social worker resolves conflicts among her responsibilities to society, client, colleagues, agency, and profession.

These seven provisions do give clues, however, to the sort of society that is being promoted. The fourth suggests a pluralistic society which encourages diversity of belief. The seventh suggests a democratic political structure, although the role of the public in "shaping social policies" is not spelled out. These principles suggest pieces of a political structure. Provisions one through three are even more revealing. They admonish the social worker to act to prevent and eliminate discrimination based on race, sex, age, etc., and to expand opportunity and choice for all persons. The second asks workers "to ensure that all persons have access to resources and services they require." These provisions suggest a liberal political program, in line with Democratic party platforms in the 1970s – programs of increased aid to the needy, of active enforcement by government of equal opportunity, and so on.

This sort of political program, however, is only suggested, not explicitly stated. One could argue that the Code is consistent with conservative Republican programs as well. What is unstated are the political and economic contexts in terms of which we are to understand discrimination, opportunity and needed resources. The National Platform of the Republican Party in 1984, for example, claimed that most of the needy already had access to resources and services, and so while we should provide for the needy and prevent discrimination, we were already effectively doing so.[12]

Section Six of the Code is the most general in its provisions. The other sections present an odd mixture of quite specific provisions and impossibly vague ones: social workers are told quite specifically that they should not solicit clients of their agency for private practice (II.F.2) and that they should not engage in sexual activities with clients (II.F.5). They are also told to "serve clients with devotion, loyalty, determination . . ." (II.F.1) and to "practice wisdom with colleagues" (V.O.3).

The Code's failure to provide an explicit ethical and political basis for social work results from laudable but questionable aims. It is to provide a rule-regulated basis and equitable procedures for disciplinary action against unethical practices. Thus there are specific provisions about solicitation of clients, sexual conduct, financial arrangements, racial discrimination, and so on.

In addition, there is a need for general guidelines that can help resolve ethical dilemmas and will bring out the unifying values of the profession. Here, the guidelines become extremely general and they do not make explicit their underlying ethical or political basis. I assume that the guidelines are this way (1) because social workers are wary of being associated with one "political line" and because they persist in the mistaken belief that "professionalism" is compatible with an apolitical or uncontroversial point of view. (2) The guidelines are also vague to preserve the fiction that agreed-upon values unite social work.

The Code presents an odd ethical stand: (1) it acknowledges that social workers constantly make ethical choices and that these choices are necessarily part of a broader ethical and political framework. It even hints at the sort of political structure it advocates, as we saw in examining provisions of the Code. (2) It remains silent, however, about any explicit political/social/ethical basis of its practice.

Some social workers have acknowledged this problem with

social work ethics and have attempted to provide the missing basis. Let us consider two of the most important recent attempts and their limitations.

Ethical bases for social work

Both C. S. Levy, in *Social Work Ethics* (1976), and F. G. Reamer, in *Ethical Dilemmas in Social Service* (1982), attempt to provide an ethical basis for social work, using the Code of Ethics as a starting point.[13] Levy's position typifies a widely-held view. Paradoxical as it sounds, he argues that the justification of the Code of Ethics is that it needs no justification.

Levy acknowledges the central importance of ethical issues in social work and the need for ethical standards. Social work ethics become "a professional standard by which individual social workers can be guided as they encounter ethical issues in their practice."[14] Levy accepts guidelines similar to those in the current Code, guidelines that designate responsibilities to clients, colleagues, profession, employer, society.

Levy argues that social work ethics is tied to service situations but should not be tied to a more general framework. He argues that ethical considerations can and should be considered separately from other contexts, including social and political contexts. He quotes Edel, who has written on educational philosophy from an existentialist standpoint, as capturing the spirit of his view:

> it is primarily an argument for the independence of ethical judgment from theological, metaphysical, and scientific, in brief any existential pictures of the world and its necessities.[15]

Levy does not elaborate on this idea, nor does he give arguments to support it. He devotes only one page to it, and does not clarify the position. He seems, however, to be arguing that ethical standards can and should be evaluated in themselves, without being tied to a philosophical world view.

There are at least two major objections to his position. The first can be made by pointing out that Levy misconstrues Edel's position. Edel, in the passage cited, is referring to twentieth-century views of ethics, and Edel himself argues against this separation of ethics from other aspects of a belief system. For Edel, beliefs about what we should do are necessarily tied to our beliefs about the nature of the world, of society, of human nature. We can only decide what we *should* do in the context of what we *can* do, what society can accomplish, etc. It is odd that Levy uses for support an argument that negates his own position.[16]

Second, even if we isolate our ethical from our other beliefs, as, for example, some forms of ethical intuitionism do, we must still justify these beliefs in terms of their underlying *ethical* basis. Levy's standards need to be justified in terms of intuitionism or utilitarianism or some such system. Because he does not indicate how the particular ethical standards are derived or justified, his account is unsatisfactory and unhelpful in just the same ways as the Code of Ethics.

Reamer's theory is much more adequate in philosophical terms and does provide ethical underpinnings for social work practice. Reamer gives a detailed account of the ways in which ethical factors enter into social work. He then argues for a particular ethical framework, which is consistent with the Code of Ethics and which he believes will be helpful in resolving conflicts. The underlying framework is based largely on Gewirth's work in philosophy.[17] It gives general principles that we can use in deciding individual cases. The basic concept is that we are responsible persons, capable of rational thought. Reamer, through Gewirth, argues that as rational, responsible persons, we are logically committed to principles of freedom and well-being, not only as necessary to ourselves but as basic rights of all persons. Thus, we are best served if we act always to secure these rights for everyone. The right to well-being is specified in terms of certain sorts of goods: simply put, we have a right to such goods as enough food to eat and adequate housing because these goods are necessary for us to act as autonomous, rational persons. Reamer then tries to show how this framework can be used in making social work decisions. Reamer's account is presented more fully in the next chapter; at this point I wish to focus on only one point.

Reamer's account provides us with one of several possible ethical frameworks, and while it is an interesting one, he does not give compelling reasons for accepting his account rather than some other. Reamer seems to assume that the framework he gives is the most plausible basis for social work and that the Code of Ethics, with some refinement, is adequate as an expression of values for the social work profession.

He needs, however, to argue more fully for these claims. Certainly, within philosophy, Gewirth's work has been greeted with objections, because it conflicts with other contemporary accounts of ethics, such as those by Rawls, Nozick and MacIntyre.[18] Further, we need to know more about the political and social structure that underlies "the rights" he advocates. His account would be greatly enhanced if he explained its relation to other frameworks and argued for its superiority over them.

Alternative theories, particularly socialist critiques, reveal the limitations of both Levy's and Reamer's accounts. (1) They acknowledge an ethical/political basis to existing social work practice; (2) they point out important contradictions within that practice; and (3) they offer an alternative ethical/political basis that would lead to a different kind of social work practice.[19]

These accounts take as their starting point goals consistent with one interpretation of the Code of Ethics. If we look at it again, particularly Section six, its broadest goals are empowerment of the client and social change directed towards that empowerment. Empowerment is strongly suggested by the statement that the worker's primary responsibility is to the client and also by the mandates to create access to needed resources and services, equal opportunity, and democratic participation in social policy and institutions. Social change is mandated by all these provisions, as well as by provision six – to improve social conditions.

Socialist accounts question whether we can achieve this kind of empowerment with our existing economic/political structure and institutions. They point out that accounts like Reamer's simply assume that our existing structure, with some modifications, is adequate for achieving these goals, without fully examining the history and the effects of these structures and institutions.

In addition, some of the socialist accounts suggest that

existing social work practice not only fails to bring about real empowerment but subtly undermines it. They make the argument that the focus on "professionalism," for example, runs the risk of increasing the power and authority of the worker over the client and thus of empowering workers rather than clients. And they argue that casework itself is in danger of focusing on the individual to the exclusion of social change.[20] Reamer does not confront the broad questions underlying these examples: can our existing institutional frameworks, including the social work profession as it is practiced, bring about the goals espoused? What are the alternatives?

The existing Code of Ethics may thus be contradictory in a second way. (1) We saw earlier that for its provisions to have any real content and to be useful they must be framed in a particular ethical/political/social structure, yet the Code never articulates any such structure. (2) In addition, if such a structure were made explicit, it might well be seen to undermine the very goals it espouses.

These contradictions may turn out to be illusory. Any examination of social work ethics, however, needs to take these issues seriously. We should not simply assume (1) that existing social work institutions and practices, even with modifications, are adequate for the goals they espouse, nor (2) that the existing Code of Ethics best expresses the goals we wish to achieve. We must consider alternative structures and accounts, including other Codes of Ethics, which may set forth different social work practices.[21]

The limitation of Levy's and Reamer's accounts is that they never engage in this sort of radical questioning; and thus their ethical systems lack the kind of justification they most need – the demonstration that in our complex and confusing world of choices we should accept their suggested guidance on ethical issues over other systems that may appear equally plausible – offered by religion, a specific community, or a philosophical work. Most glaringly, they do not justify their approach in light of the kind of socialist critique just outlined.

An alternative proposal

My proposal emerges from what I see as shortcomings in the alternatives described in the preceding section. Instead of developing yet another ethical framework for social work, I would like to suggest a different way of thinking about the ethical issues. Since social work decisions require an underlying framework (my point against Levy), and since there are several frameworks to choose from (my point against Reamer), then social workers should engage in dialogue about alternative frameworks. Social workers should acknowledge the diversity of ethical views that confront them and set aside time for examining them. Each social worker must determine her own position – the sort of social worker she will be. As I shall argue in subsequent chapters, only with a developed political and ethical framework can a worker adequately resolve particular dilemmas on such matters as confidentiality or coercion of clients.

To develop an informed ethical position, however, a social worker needs the opportunity to compare different ethical views in relation to cases. Until now, books on social work ethics have usually either analyzed general frameworks apart from particular cases, or have analyzed cases using one ethical framework.[22] Social workers have thus received little useful help in making ethical decisions. By considering cases in relation to conflicting ethical frameworks, each social worker can develop an informed position that is relevant to her daily practice. In addition, such an approach will reveal the limitations of philosophical analyses that remain remote from people's actual experiences.

My point of view, then, is that *dialogue* is central to ethics. Only through sustained and open dialogue can we develop informed ethical positions. Dialogue of this sort assumes (1) that we can communicate across different views; (2) that we can be open to each other; and (3) that we need other views in order to fully reexamine our own. Dialogue of this sort is itself an ethic, best exemplified in the early works of Plato, where Socrates questions the actions and views of his fellow citizens and urges them to rethink what they are doing. The dialogues often end without a conclusion, the conclusion being that we must constantly reexamine our answers.

It would be naive and misleading to suppose, however, that my approach does not itself presuppose other ethical, political, and social commitments. I shall sketch some of my assumptions here and will elaborate on them more fully in the next chapter.

I assume that social workers are committed to achieving the broad goals outlined in the Code of Ethics – goals of empowerment of the client and social change directed towards that empowerment. While "empowerment" is vague, I shall assume that it includes respect and dignity of the individual, access to basic goods and services, equal opportunity, and participation in the political and social decisions of the society, as the Code stipulates.

I assume that there is fundamental disagreement in the society about the best way to achieve these goals, and disagreement within the social work community itself. Throughout the book, I suggest in a variety of ways the need for debate about these disagreements. Only in this way can we fully examine the plurality of views that confronts us and arrive at better ways of thinking about ethics.

In examining different cases, particular attention will be paid to inconsistencies in current social work practice. I argue that some dominant social work practices undermine the goals social workers espouse, and in this I borrow from critiques made by socialist social workers. This sort of contradiction requires that a social worker reexamine current practice and the alternatives to it. This book is meant to help in that process by offering the opportunity to examine case decisions in light of the political and moral commitments they presuppose.

Before turning to case decisions, however, we need a better understanding of the different ethical perspectives that characterize our "pluralist" culture and so confusingly permeate our decisions. Chapter 2 will describe some of these basic perspectives.

2 Unraveling ethical assumptions

"He who would do good to another, must do it in Minute Particulars. General Good is the plea of the scoundrel, hypocrite and flatterer."[1]

Why do we need an ethical perspective?

Although "ethics" is sometimes distinguished from "morality;" I shall use the terms interchangeably to refer to THE SYSTEMATIC EXPLORATION OF QUESTIONS ABOUT HOW WE SHOULD ACT IN RELATION TO OTHERS.[2]

Consider, for example, a decision to go back to school for an advanced degree in social work. Suppose that someone presses you to explain why.

– Why are you doing this?
– I want better training for working with adolescents.
– Why? You're already a very skilled worker.
– Well, then I'll get promoted.
– Why do you want that?
– Then I'll get better salary.
– Why is that important?
– Then I can send my kids to college.
– Why is that important?
– Well, education is valuable in itself and I want my kids to have that experience.

Another person might have answered the questions differently:

– Why are you doing this?
– I want more training.
– Why? You're already a very skilled worker.
– Well, I want the promotion.
– Why?
– I'll have more power and then I'll really be able to help people.
– Why is that important?

– Well, I guess I believe that every person should have an equal chance in society to be happy and deserves to be treated with respect and dignity.

Through this kind of questioning, we learn more about our own and others' moral viewpoints. The questions reveal that our decisions are based on some sort of guidelines, that we do not act in a vacuum. Our actions are influenced by precepts we were taught as children, expectations of society and profession, as well as by our own goals. Our actions will reflect these different forces, even though we may not always understand them. If we decide to go back to school, we do so on the basis of some reason, ill-formulated as it may be, or of some social force or custom we have accepted. If we refuse to let clients see their case records, we are also operating on some sort of guideline. We may have a quite explicit belief that effective help requires secrecy about diagnosis and treatment plan, or we may be acting on an unquestioned habit of following the rules of our agency. When asked for our reasons, we are forced to consider the hidden assumptions behind our behavior.

At some point, the questioning will end, because we have reached a fundamental principle or reason beyond which we do not know what to say. But even the final answers pose ethical questions for us.

(1) *What do we mean by the concepts we use to explain our actions?* Do we understand what commitments we are making by our stated beliefs in "equality" or "happiness" or "helping effectively"? We need to explain these concepts more fully.

(2) *In what general framework do these concepts and principles fit?* Once we start to explain our actions, often we discover that we are acting on conflicting reasons. You might return to school, for example, both to help others more effectively and to further your career. Yet in some situations helping others may conflict with pursuing career interests. You may be asked to direct a newly funded program which you believe is not in the best interests of clients, though it is one from which you could learn a great deal and move on to a more powerful position. What should you do? Which of your interests should have priority? Is there a general framework which can help to make sense of your different actions and beliefs?

If we ignore these broader questions, we run the risk of

undermining our own goals. Take, for example, the case presented in the last chapter. Suppose the worker sees the family for several months and they come to trust and depend on her. Then, without informing them, she discusses the case with a worker from yet another agency involved with the family. The mother feels betrayed, since she has had some legitimate problems with the other agency, and the worker thereby destroys the trust she has worked hard to establish. If one action conveys trust and another action undermines it, we are acting at cross purposes and may seriously harm clients. So, also, if some actions help clients and others promote our careers at clients' expense, we again contradict ourselves. Only if we develop a coherent perspective can we have any assurance that we will act with moral integrity and with the seriousness required by our power over others' lives.

We will focus on a series of questions, intended to reveal the complex variety of assumptions that enter into actual decisions:

(1) What are my goals in this case and in this agency?
(2) What choice is required in this case?
(3) What is the client's point of view?
(4) What are the alternative courses of action?
(5) What positions do these different alternatives represent?
(6) How should I handle differences between my client's and my own position?
(7) Is the solution consistent with my original goals?

One important implication of this approach is that "political" and "ethical" issues must be treated together. Traditionally, ethics is defined in terms of what a person ought to do in relation to others – what constitutes right action or the good in life, while politics is defined in terms of how a society ought to be – what structure of government and of society enables a group to function best. Since, however, a person's good is inextricably linked to the structure and functioning of the society, the two cannot be examined separately. For example, in considering the "good" of a client, the nature of the relationship commits you to some view of altruism and rights which entails assumptions about what society, and the government in particular, owes its citizens. These factors significantly influence us, whether we choose to recognize them or not.

In the next section, a case will be used to examine some of the ethical and political perspectives that influence social work decisions.

Ethical theories: a case

Sometimes a moral choice will dramatically reveal more than one moral perspective. Consider the following case:

> You are a supervisor of caseworkers in a shelter for the homeless. The shelter accommodates about seventy persons and provides food, lodging, and social services until clients can be placed more permanently, hopefully within three months. Once placed, primary responsibility is shifted from the shelter to the mental health agency in the catchment area, and the shelter is then able to take in new homeless persons.
>
> For a particular client, call her Doris, you have found placement in a half-way house in a city suburb, with follow-up services at the area's mental health center. Doris is told, as are all clients, that if she does not stay with the program, you cannot take her back.
>
> This policy was instituted because it encourages mental health clinics to take responsibility for the clients transferred to them and encourages clients to stay with their programs. If the mental health clinic knows the shelter will take back its former clients, then the clinic will sometimes terminate the client as soon as there are difficulties, particularly since clinics are reluctant to take the more difficult homeless clients in the first place. The policy enables the shelter to assure secure placement for the largest number of homeless and to encourage mental health agencies to assume full responsibility for clients they receive.
>
> Suppose, however, that you know that Doris may well drop out of the program because neither this nor any existing program fits her needs. Suppose she does drop out. She is

again homeless and in need of help. Should you readmit her to the shelter?

This decision can be posed as a conflict between two prominent theories: Kantian and utilitarian ethics.

Utilitarianism focuses on the consequences of our actions, on acting to bring about the maximum happiness (or minimum pain) in the society as a whole: we should always aim for the overall happiness of the community and not for that of any particular individual. By contrast, Kantianism focuses on a fundamental dignity each and every person possesses as a rational being. We ought always to act with respect for that rational dignity, regardless of the consequences of our actions for the society as a whole. On one reading of the Kantian position, we should take Doris back into the program, for our duty is to treat her with the respect and dignity owed to every person. On a utilitarian view, however, we should stick to our policy, because that will seemingly lead to the greatest overall benefit to society.

While these descriptions are oversimplified, they convey a basic difference of approach which results in different resolutions of our case. The two theories have been influential in the way we think about ethics today, and disagreements about cases often reveal a tension between them.

I shall sketch some of the central features of each theory in order to convey something of its particular way of thinking about ethics and its limitations for human service cases. Four other ethical perspectives will then be presented, because they too influence our decisions, whether we realize it or not: rights-based, Marxist-based, virtue-based perspectives, and intuitionism. Each of the theories represents a way that people think about our relationships and responsibilities in the world. Through understanding the different views, and analyzing their strengths and weaknesses, we can better evaluate our own vision of morality.

I Utilitarianism[3]

Utilitarianism developed in part as a corrective to the inequalities and suffering present in eighteenth- and nineteenth-century European and English societies. By the eighteenth century, the medieval, hierarchical social order had largely broken down. The authority of the monarchy itself was being eroded, and religion was no longer the unquestioned source of moral authority. Instead there was a new interest in morality based on rational deliberation, apart from religion. A new middle class was becoming more powerful. Industrialization was developing and with it the problems of urban crowding, a new kind of poverty, industrial hazards, unemployment on a large scale, etc.

The greatest exponents of utilitarianism, Jeremy Bentham and John Stuart Mill, were at heart social reformers. They were both actively engaged in numerous legal and penal reforms throughout their lives. Their work was based on the goal of promoting the general welfare – the maximum happiness of all. This goal still lies at the heart of most human service work today. Let us examine the perspective more closely.

The basic tenet of utilitarianism is that we should always act to bring about the greatest amount of good or happiness, or the least amount of harm in the world as a whole. This includes several important assumptions.

(1) The *good of society* is the sum of the good of the individuals in it. If we act for the greatest happiness of all individuals, we will thereby create the best society.

(2) The greatest happiness will include both immediate consequences of an action and foreseeable, long-term consequences. We should evaluate actions solely in terms of their consequences: they are means to the end of promoting general welfare.

(3) If an individual's calculation of greatest happiness is a *rational, deliberative* process, then the result will be a basic agreement about the nature of happiness.

  (a) My rational consideration of very different sorts of happiness – the pleasure of drunkenness versus the pleasure of an intellectual life – will lead to choosing the rational or "higher" happiness.

  (b) When my happiness appears to conflict with yours, a rational calculation will result in understanding that our long-term interests are not at odds. Thus, for example, while I may initially want to provide few services to the poor, so as to keep my taxes low, I may come to see that my happiness lies in higher taxes and more benefits to the poor: they will then become productive citizens and contribute more fully to the welfare of all, which in the end will give me more money.

(c) Education of all citizens is essential to bringing about general welfare. Education will enable us to shape our desires rationally – to understand that much of what we initially view as happiness would not make us happy. Through education, our desires develop so as to become what is truly desirable.

(4) Human nature is such that we are naturally competitive with others. Our competitiveness is tempered, however, by our rational self-interest.

(5) Since the happiness of any one individual counts the same as that of any other, the perspective is democratic in treating everyone's welfare on an equal basis.

(6) Altruism is viewed as mutual self-interest: in the long run, promoting our own interests will also promote those of others. This leaves open the possibility of different views of altruism, depending on how one constructs "rational interest." On one view, all we need do is act in our own rational self-interest, and others' interests will thereby be promoted. On another, an individual's rational self-interest is predicated on the individual actively seeking out ways to help others.

Let us return to our case-study. Traditionally, utilitarians have been particularly concerned about such social problems as homelessness. An increasing number of people in our society today are without employment, food, housing, or medical care. Some urgently need psychiatric services, having been prematurely released from mental hospitals. To integrate them in some way back into society, legislation has been passed to set up shelters and agencies: in theory, the social worker helps "homeless" persons to become useful members of society and protects the rest of us from their unhappiness. Through such work, they thus contribute to the general welfare.

In our particular agency, rules are set up to assure shelter to the maximum number of persons. The rule not to readmit the homeless is said to be necessary to assure that others will be given shelter. In the long run, the greatest good will result:

other agencies will take full responsibility for the clients placed with them and the homeless will thereby receive the services they need.

While the case brings out the strengths of utilitarianism, it also reveals its weaknesses. The principle of maximizing happiness is so general and vague that it can be applied in quite opposite ways. One might argue, for example, that the greatest happiness is served by doing as little as possible for the homeless. Indeed, that is what has been done so far. They are a relatively small group, and many may be an unemployable "underclass" for whom it would be very costly to provide.

Nothing in utilitarianism guarantees that such a minority will be protected, if we determine that the greatest happiness lies elsewhere. Utilitarianism thus appears to have a built-in sort of injustice that runs counter to some of our deepest intuitive notions about morality. In the extreme case, we would not think it right to sacrifice an innocent bystander (lynching an innocent man, for example) no matter what happiness resulted for the majority.

In cases such as these, we can argue endlessly about how to calculate the greatest happiness: can the happiness of everyone really be promoted if individuals are mistreated? Will our "real" interests be served by higher taxes with more services for the poor, by lower taxes with fewer services for everyone, or what? While rational deliberation is supposed to result in our agreeing on what would maximize happiness, there is no such agreement. It is not clear how a large amount of happiness for, say, 80 per cent of the population is to be measured against a smaller amount of happiness for 20 per cent. Should we maximize the average happiness of human beings or the total happiness?

We cannot in fact *measure happiness*, because it includes such different sorts of things – ultimately different ways of life. How does one calculate the happiness of Mother Theresa and compare it to the happiness of Bill Cosby, Ronald Reagan, or your contented neighbor down the street? Ways of living are so different that a scale of happiness to compare them does not make sense.

If we cannot agree on a calculation of greatest happiness, then the perspective cannot provide a rational resolution of conflicts of interest on the basis of happiness. If I believe happiness will result from lowering taxes and doing less for the poor but you believe otherwise, then appealing to a principle of maximum happiness will not settle our dispute. Utilitarianism will not serve the purpose for which it was constructed. It fails to tell us what to do about the homeless or what to do about Doris.

This sort of problem gives ethics a bad reputation: when we explore the perspective, we find that it is not any real help in deciding particular cases and sometimes even runs counter to what we intuitively know to be moral.

The limitations of the perspective, however, are themselves instructive. They help us understand pitfalls in creating a viable ethical perspective and serve to warn us of the dangers of our utilitarian rules: without appropriate qualifications, utilitarianism can be destructive and can result in actions that are clearly unethical.

One other limitation of utilitarianism should be mentioned here, because of its importance for human service work. The focus on *individual* happiness ignores *institutional* forces which create unhappiness: in particular, the ways in which bureaucracies may promote their own, rather than clients', interests. In the case of the homeless, the rule against readmitting Doris may be promoted, not from concern for the long-term interests of the homeless, but so that the agency can close more cases – a need to protect the agency. "Utility" becomes narrowly construed and used to serve the purposes of bureaucratic organization, all under a banner of promoting general welfare.

Finally, however, we must not lose sight of the perspective's appeal. It captures one central moral insight: we should act so as to increase general welfare and to maximize happiness.

II Duty-based Kantianism[4]

The most famous duty-based theory is Kantian ethics, and it predates the utilitarians. Kant rejects any religious formulation for our moral beliefs. He also contributes to others' skepticism by his treatment of proofs for God's existence. Like the utilitarians, he searched for a rational justification of morality and like the utilitarians looked for it in the moral beliefs of the "common man," rather than in the relationship to God. Unlike the utilitarians, however, he believed happiness to be an unreliable guide for morality, because our notions of happiness are so changeable and so dependent on external circumstances.

Kant focused instead on a fundamental respect and dignity owed to every individual and tried to convey it in a principle called the categorical imperative:

> Always act so as to treat humanity, whether in your own person or in that of others, as an end and not as a means.

He is saying that all human beings, by virtue of their rational nature, deserve to be treated as fully rational, as we ourselves wish to be treated. Kant attempted to clarify this principle and to demonstrate its universal and binding nature by adding a second formulation:

> Act only on that maxim which you can at the same time will to be a universal law.

If I am deciding whether to act in a certain way, I should only do so if it makes sense for everyone to act on the same guideline which I am using. The exact nature of the principle becomes clearer in application, and Kant used "promising" as one of his chief illustrations.

> Another man finds himself forced by need to borrow money. He well knows that he will not be able to repay it, but he also sees that nothing will be loaned him if he does not firmly promise to repay it at a certain time. He desires to make such a promise but he has enough conscience to ask himself whether it is not improper and opposed to duty to relieve his distress in such a way.[5]

Kant argues that breaking such a promise is immoral, because in so acting we would be accepting the following maxim: "Anyone can promise what he pleases with the intention of not fulfilling it." Such a maxim would destroy itself: it would be self-contradictory because it both advocates and destroys promising. "No one would believe what was promised to him but would only laugh at such assertion as vain pretense."[6] We would thus be contradicting ourselves and the concept of promising would be destroyed.

Immediately, however, there are problems with the applications of Kant's principle. What sorts of generalizations are allowable? If breaking a promise is formulated in a different way, then it may be acceptable. Take again the example of a man borrowing money he cannot repay. Suppose that his maxim is that a promise can be broken if and only if some great harm will result from keeping the promise. The maxim does not appear to advocate the destruction of all promises and trust; it isn't clear that its universal acceptance would result in the meaninglessness of all promises.

Kant goes on to make room for even greater differences in the way we generalize from our actions. He states that our duty is also to refrain from actions which, if generalized, would be self-destructive rules. For example, he argues that we should help others who suffer great hardships. If we do not, we will be acting self-destructively, since we all may require help at some time.

This view of altruism may appear similar to the utilitarian view, in that both refer to self-interest. The two views, however, differ significantly. For utilitarians, if we act on our own rational self-interest, we will thereby act altruistically. For Kantians, altruism is a *duty* we owe to others who are suffering great hardships, whether or not it is in our interests.

One of the chief problems with Kant's account of ethics is that he does not tell us how to construct the maxims he recommends – whether, for example, we should always help others or help others only when certain other conditions prevail.

In the case of Doris, his account does not tell us what we should do. A Kantian might argue that to deny Doris readmission to the program is to treat her as a means – it is sacrificing her well-being to create a better overall program. We have a duty to treat Doris with respect and dignity and not as a means to accomplishing some greater good. To put this another way, if we universalize our refusal to care for Doris, we have a society in which people do not care for others, and this is undesirable. In doing this we would contradict ourselves, because we all need the love and sympathy of others at times. On the basis of the categorical imperative, it seems that we should take Doris back into the shelter.

On the other hand, it might be argued that if we universalize our action of readmitting Doris and thus always take back the homeless, then the local mental health clinics may cease to take full responsibility for them. In addition, one might argue that we can only treat Doris with the dignity she deserves if we hold her fully responsible for her actions. Further, we must consider more than our treatment of Doris. In readmitting her, we may be showing disrespect to another client who has been interviewed to take Doris's place.

Even though the theory does not give us a clear moral basis for action, it has a strong appeal. It is reminiscent of other more familiar ethical sayings: "Do unto others as you would they should do unto you" or "What would happen if everyone did that." It makes us focus on the value of every individual person and on the respect owed to a person, apart from that person's usefulness and apart from our own desires, a respect essential to human dignity and one easily undermined in human service settings. It does not, however, help us to resolve our particular case dilemmas.

Part of the appeal of both theories is the simplicity of their structures, yet that very simplicity seems to make them unsatisfactory in practice. They fail to capture the complexities with which human service workers are continually faced.

The theories leave us with three central problems. (1) In application, each theory can be used to justify conflicting actions. There are utilitarian and Kantian arguments on both sides of the issue of readmitting Doris. (2) Neither theory adequately specifies its more general social/political context. Each specifies a process of individual decision-making which will lead to right action. Neither specifies the sorts of institutions and political structures within which right actions fit. (3) Finally, neither theory can tell us how to decide between them. Each theory has its strengths and weaknesses, and any criteria we use other than logical consistency will bring in yet other ethical assumptions which need justification.

Let us turn to two other perspectives, important in human service work today.

III Rights-based theories[7]

Both utilitarianism and Kantianism assume that people have some important ethical and political beliefs in common and so are able to agree at a basic level about what is good. Utilitarianism assumes that there will be fundamental agreement about what counts as "happiness" and that one person's "rational" happiness is not radically at odds with another's. Kantianism assumes that we agree about the basic requirements a society must meet in order for people to be treated with respect and dignity.

Rights-based theories, on the other hand, usually assume that there are widely differing views within a society about what is good and about the sort of society that can best achieve that good. These theories have traditionally focused on protecting an individual's freedom from encroachment by others – freedom rights. Society is viewed not as a community of common interests but more as a battleground of different interests, where the individual's freedom and interests must be balanced against those of others. The only common value is freedom itself – freedom to act in particular ways or freedom to be protected from the arbitrary actions of others.

To determine what freedoms we should have and how society should be structured, we must consider what our lives would be like without any social or legal restrictions – in a supposed "state of nature." The assumption is that in such a state we would all act for our particular self-interest, for example, acquiring whatever we could or mistreating others if it were to our benefit. Others would act in similar ways toward us, so while we would all have a maximum amount of freedom, we would have no security – no peace, no arbiter of conflict, no rules.

To escape this way of life, people come together to form a *social contract*: they agree to give up some of their freedom in exchange for a different sort – freedom from the arbitrary actions of others. Those forming the contract create "the state" which alone has the right to use force but only to enforce the new protections of, and restrictions on, freedom.

The basic tenets of rights-based theories can be sketched as follows:

(1) The good society is one which protects the rational autonomy of every individual through maximizing the extent of individual freedom consistent with justice for all.

(2) Freedom is defined by rights: *freedom rights* are guarantees of non-interference by the state or others in an individual's exercise of actions essential to his or her autonomy, actions such as owning property or expressing oneself in public. *Entitlement rights* are guarantees of state action to preserve an individual's autonomy, for example, guarantees of health care or a minimum standard of education.
(3) The state is a politically neutral instrument whose major tasks are to guarantee rights and to protect citizens from external threat.
(4) Human beings are essentially rational individuals; each is equal to any other in rationality, and society is viewed as the sum of all individuals within it.
(5) In exercising their rationality, individuals can best determine their particular happiness.

These basic tenets suggest a key question for a rights-based theory: how do we decide what rights we have? A rights-based theory must be able to justify the rights it proposes on the basis of some more fundamental principle or principles. It must show that a society based on the rights it proposes is one in which we can all live the best sort of life.

There are fundamental disagreements among rights theorists about the rights we have and about the sort of society and government which will promote them. The homeless provide a good example of the depth of the disagreements.

The implication of some rights theories is that the homeless do not have a right to housing or to other services such as health care or a minimum income. At best, these are provided from our sense of charity. Some libertarians, for example, argue that the role of government is primarily to protect individuals from the encroachment of others, including encroachment by the government. Each individual should pursue his or her interests with minimal restraints. On this view, the market economy and competition will lead to the most equitable distribution of resources. Our primary entitlements in society are those that we have acquired or earned.[8]

From the viewpoint of other rights theories, the homeless are entitled to housing and other services. Some "liberals" argue that the role of government is to ensure to individuals the basic requirements of a good life, not simply to protect what we have acquired or earned. These basic requirements include food, shelter, health care, etc. All individuals have a right to these goods, if they are unable to acquire them. Justice is thus based on equality with respect to basic goods. The market economy must be regulated by the government to rectify disparities in income and to create equality of opportunity to compete. On this view, the homeless do have a right to housing.[9]

Let us consider one rights theory in more detail. Reamer's book, *Ethical Dilemmas in Social Service*, provides one of the few serious attempts to present a rights theory as a basis for social work practice and to show how it would apply in particular cases.[10]

Borrowing heavily from Gewirth, Reamer argues for ethical guidelines which would justify traditional social work values.[11] The theory centers on basic rights of freedom and well-being, which are derived logically from the features of rational action. Gewirth and Reamer attempt to show that any person, by virtue of his or her rationality, is committed to freedom and well-being as not only necessary for the individual but also as basic rights of all persons. In deciding what to do, you should "Act in accord with the generic rights of your recipients [the agents of one's actions] as well as of yourself."[12] Well-being consists of three sorts of goods: (1) *Basic goods* provide the preconditions for action. Without these goods (such as life and health and mental equilibrium) we cannot act as rational persons in the world. The second and third are less basic and therefore harder to justify as rights. They do not follow clearly from the features of rational action. (2) *Non-subtractive goods* are those whose loss would diminish one's strivings (for example, without truth-telling we cannot act effectively in the world). (3) *Additive goods* are those which would enhance one's ability to fulfill one's purposes (such as knowledge and income).[13]

This perspective helps little in Doris's case. We might decide the homeless have rights that are not being honored – the right to housing, health, mental equilibrium. We still have to decide, however, whether or not to readmit Doris. And although her rights are being violated, so are others who need a place in the center.

In addition, Reamer does not make clear enough what goods are necessary. Even with basic goods, which are the preconditions of action, we need to know more about what would count as providing "mental equilibrium" or how far that good is to be balanced against another person's well-being, a person who is paying high taxes to help provide for another's mental equilibrium. The limits of nonsubtractive and additive goods are even less clear. Reamer inherits some of the problems of balancing different sorts of good that we found in utilitarianism.

Also, Reamer does not give us reasons for accepting his account over other competing ethical approaches. While he tries to show the theory's superiority over utilitarianism, he does not explain why it should be preferred over other accounts of rights, such as by Rawls or Nozick. It provides us with one framework, which we need to compare with others. He has not provided compelling reasons why the social work profession as a whole should accept this one theory over alternatives to it.

From this brief account, we can see both the appeal and limitations of rights-based theories. They are appealing, because they seem to provide an ethical framework for a society like ours in which there is wide disagreement on ethical, political, religious, and metaphysical issues. According to rights theorists, we can agree to disagree – everyone should have certain freedoms to think and act differently from others. The problem is that a rights-based theory must itself make political, ethical, and metaphysical assumptions, among which we must decide. The differences in rights-based theories sometimes appear as fundamental as those between utilitarian and Kantian frameworks.

IV Marxist-based ethical frameworks[14]

Marxist-based frameworks are usually viewed as primarily political, rather than ethical. These theories, however, while almost always more explicit about their political assumptions, would not make sense without some sort of assumed ethics. Thus, they have the inverse problem of rights-based theories, which are explicit about their ethical claims but leave unstated many of their equally important political and social assumptions.

Because they play an increasingly important role in the world today and provide important critiques of human service work, Marxist-based ethical frameworks are included here. These theories pose two chief difficulties for the task of sketching their basic tenets. (1) They differ widely among themselves, particularly if one includes the whole range of socialist theories. (2) They focus almost exclusively on broad societal changes which are often remote from the daily activities of social workers. With these qualifications in mind, the following gives a brief sketch of some of the most important tenets of this ethical perspective:

(1) The good society is a continually developing one with social and economic institutions that create respect, freedom, and equality for all persons.
(2) The essence of being human and of being free does not reside in a person's rationality (as for Kant and Mill) but in a person's *activity* or *praxis* – the person's transformation of the world through purposeful labor. Creative, purposeful labor is the basis of human fulfillment and happiness.
    (a) The specific form of labor in a society (the mode of production) determines the fundamental features of the society and the nature of its inhabitants.
    (b) Thus, ethics and human nature and rationality are *historical* products.
(3) Most modes of production (including capitalism) divide society into two opposing classes which compete for scarce resources. This results in the domination of one class over the other and in the alienation of all individuals within the society. Alienation is an individual's isolation from other individuals – the loss of human cooperativeness and of creative labor.
(4) Freedom and respect of all individuals can only come about if the mode of production is socialized – that is, if:
    (a) cooperation replaces competition;
    (b) no one group has significant economic, social, or political power over any other group;
    (c) the mode of production is controlled by those doing the work.
(5) "Socialized" production will result in a new human nature, in democratic process, and in equal opportunity for all.
(6) Altruism will exist only in the form of *reciprocal* giving.

While Marx gave a powerful and compelling account of the ways in which our capitalist system oppresses us, his and other socialist accounts are much more vague about ethical guidelines or ideals. And they are deliberately so: the nature of the desirable society can only be determined when the capitalist mode of production and social relations have been transformed.

We can thus only say in quite general ways what this perspective suggests for ethics. Our actions must be directed at recognizing the ways in which we are divided against each other and made powerless or powerful. We must work to change the structure of the economy and social relations, so that power is more equally distributed. The focus, then, is on social change. In human service work, this would include working towards more reciprocal relationships between client and worker, more democratic decision-making processes, and more resources available to the poor.

Let us try to apply this perspective in Doris's case. The account makes clear that we must work not just to help Doris but to create a society in which homelessness is not a problem. We can use Doris's situation to pressure the state for more homeless shelters, to organize political action in the agency, perhaps even to organize clients themselves. We should try to use Doris's situation to gain more control for workers and clients in the agency. Primarily, we should use the situation to educate others: (1) about ways we are divided against each other – agency against agency, client against worker; (2) and more generally about ways our economic system, based on profit, results in mental facilities that leave many people without housing or food or other needed services.

But while these actions are important and their value hard to dispute, they focus on long-term change for the homeless and do not help us with Doris *now*. Most Marxist accounts of human services, because of their focus on political issues, have sorely neglected the immediate context. In Doris's case, working for social change should not be at the expense of sacrificing Doris or the worker. Marxist accounts sometimes seem to suggest actions that ignore the immediate needs of clients or make impossible demands on workers who themselves have real concerns about maintaining their jobs.

In addition, these accounts have not adequately addressed

serious theoretical issues that are central to social work ethics. How, for example, do we justify individual rights in an ethical system that advocates the elimination of individualism? With persons who require full-time care, such as the severely mentally retarded, how do we create reciprocity between client and worker? Given that both workers and clients are primarily women, and both are underprivileged in the society, how can a worker act so as to empower both herself and her client? The analysis of sexism must be better integrated into the analysis of class. In summary, the daily ethical decisions – of confidentiality, allocating resources, taking children out of the home – should form a central part of Marxist analyses of human service.

V Intuitionist ethical theories[15]

Every ethical perspective is based on intuition. In formulating our goals we must ultimately rely on our moral intuitions of what is right or good. We evaluate ethical perspectives in part by applying to them "obvious" cases of right action to see if they promote or at least allow for these cases. In so doing, we attempt to shape and refine our moral intuitions in a rational way.

"Intuitionism," however, also refers to a particular sort of ethical perspective. There are several different ones, but common to all of them is the belief that there is no rational system by which we can order conflicting moral factors and no general theory or rules by which every case can be decided. Instead, we must consider and weigh the different factors involved and then act on the basis of what we intuitively decide is best.

The appeal of this approach is that it enables us to act flexibly without "sacrificing" a client to a moral principle. In some situations, we may have a "gut" feeling that we must, say, preserve confidentiality, even though we cannot find an adequate justification. This fits our sentiment that moral concerns cannot always be articulated and that we must ultimately rely on basic intuitive feelings about what is right.

The weakness of the approach is that we may find ourselves acting on the basis of prejudice or personal whim. How do we know what particular intuitions are true ones? An intuition which at the moment of decision seems certain and infallible is often revealed in retrospect as the misguided judgment it was.

Advocates of this approach appear to have given up the attempt to find a rational basis by which we can decide ethical issues. Instead, ethics becomes a matter of individual intuitions. This ethical framework thus raises for us the same question that different ethical frameworks together pose: how do we decide among them? If there are no criteria we can use to establish that one approach is better than another, then won't our ethical decisions be arbitrary and subjective? Is there any point then to thinking about ethics? We shall turn to these questions later in this chapter.

VI Virtue-based frameworks[16]

Virtue-based frameworks provide the most familiar way of thinking about morality. Most of the time we do not think about our moral decisions in terms of upholding rights, maximizing happiness or universalizing our actions; we more usually speak of moral qualities in ourselves and others which we desire or reject – qualities such as generosity, sensitivity, truthfulness, humor, loyalty, mean-spiritedness, deviousness, selfishness. These qualities define our relationships to others.

Psychiatry and psychiatric social work have always focused on the relationship as the key to making people "better," although the ethical framework has not usually been made explicit or clear. There has been renewed interest in this approach to ethics in some philosophical circles and there is a long tradition of virtue-based ethical theories, as well. Although most philosophers still ignore it, the framework plays a major role for many people who consider themselves practicing Christians, Jews, and Moslems.

Like rights-based theories, virtue-based theories have different formulations, from Plato up to recent work of A. MacIntyre.[17] The theories are alike, however, in their claim that the goal of action is human excellence, which is identified with the possession of virtues. Virtues are qualities of character, such as generosity, truthfulness, or compassion. They are habitual, rational ways of acting, which are considered good in themselves because they partly constitute what it is to be a good person. The rationale for being honest is not because it will lead to some good result (honesty pays or honesty will result in a good society); rather, being honest is itself a human excellence and part of what it is to be a good person.

Our most familiar examples of this approach to ethics today come from religion, and in our culture from Christianity and Judaism. For Christians, the goal of action is human excellence – purification of the soul or life in accord with the divine. The key virtues are compassion and love of God. These virtues, and others like humility, truthfulness, friendship, or generosity, define our relations to others and in part define the sort of society into which these virtues fit. Even within Christianity there have been different conceptions of the virtuous person and these reflect different social and political assumptions. In the early Christianity of the first century, for example, a key virtue was loving God through mutual sharing and humility, a virtue important in the communities of Christians reacting against the social excesses of the Roman Empire. This picture of human excellence contrasts sharply with an early Protestant one in which acquisition of goods and thriftiness were signs of one's salvation.

In Judaism, there has always been a strong emphasis on good works *in this life*. For a long time the only sort of immortality was that of the continued existence of the community itself. The life of the community was primary: connectedness to others; the centrality of daily observance of religious ritual; and the continuation of the religious tradition. Virtues which promoted these concerns were emphasized: wisdom, learnedness in spiritual and secular matters, compassion, charity, love of God.[18]

I have used Christianity and Judaism as examples of virtue-based theories because they figure prominently in many people's lives in this country and are the basis of much human service work – Alcoholics Anonymous, American Friends Service Committee, B'nai Brith, Jewish Community Services, and so on. In addition, many people who explicitly reject Christianity or Judaism retain the concepts of a virtue-based framework in making moral choices. There have even been some attempts recently to construct new non-religious, virtue-based frameworks, as in the work of I. Murdoch and A. MacIntyre.

This approach to ethics is appealing, because it reflects questions that most of us see as central to our daily lives: what should my relationship be to my family, my friends, my co-workers, my neighbors, strangers? What sort of person should I be? What sort of integrity does my life reveal?

Virtue-based theories, however, reflect different concepts of human excellence and of human society, and the social and political assumptions are not always made explicit. Aristotle's concept of the good person was of a rich Athenian gentleman and we cannot fully understand this apart from the context of the highly stratified society of fourth-century Athens. In rejecting that concept of human excellence, with virtues that only great wealth makes possible, we are also rejecting certain political or social arrangements. As already pointed out, Christianity gives us several different concepts of human excellence, from the humble servant of God to the industrious reaper of earthly success, and these too depend on social and political assumptions about how society ought to be structured. We are again confronted by the question of how we should decide which virtue-based framework to accept and thus also what political and social arrangements to strive for.

Today, we have inherited bits and pieces of several of these earlier frameworks, without any sense of a coherent picture of human excellence and without any sense of the political/social arrangements which would complete the picture. Thus we may praise virtues of thrift and generosity, charity and self-actualization, obedience and autonomy, humility and ambitiousness, without any notion of whether they are compatible.

This is further complicated by our notion of a "professional" person and issues of "professional ethics." A virtue-based ethics seems particularly appropriate to professions, because the ethical issues so often focus on the nature of the relationships and our responsibilities in those relationships – to the client, other colleagues, our supervisors, the agency itself. What sort of person ought a "professional" social worker to be? What is human excellence in that context?

In their descriptions of a social worker's responsibilities, textbooks suggest such virtues as compassion, detached caring, warmth, and honesty. Some additional virtues would also seem particularly appropriate: a certain kind of moral courage, hopefulness (an important and neglected virtue), and humility.[19]

In a professional context, however, these virtues are not considered valuable in themselves but solely as a means of helping the client or achieving the agency's goals.[20] Thus, it could be argued that if some other way of acting would help the client more (lying to a client or being less compassionate), these actions would be taken instead. This raises questions about how we are to understand the professional relationship. It seems to combine conflicting goals which are not compatible and which can thus be confusing to both worker and client.

If we return to the case of Doris, our homeless client, we must ask what sort of relationship should exist between worker and client? The worker is asked to combine a caring concern, which requires her to take Doris back into the shelter, with a professional objectivity, which requires her to stick to the agency's policy. How can these different roles be combined?

If we adopt a virtue-based ethical framework, we must reexamine the professional relationship to understand more fully the sorts of responsibilities we are undertaking and the concept of human excellence we are promoting, not only in our goals for the client, but in our goals as social workers. If our goal for the client is autonomy and honesty, to take two qualities, yet the relationship fosters dependence and is not itself always honest, then we are confronted with an important contradiction. These issues will be taken up in Chapter 7.

Approach of this book

Any introduction to ethics is itself a particular ethical point of view. Even in the way questions are posed, one makes assumptions about the proper domain of ethics and its limits. Thus, in what I have presented so far I have offered a perspective which should be made more explicit.

The central question, "how ought we to act in relation to others?" suggests the primacy of relationships in understanding ethics. Some textbooks choose instead to describe ethics in terms of principles of conduct governing an individual or a profession.

Part of my argument is that principles – like those of utilitarianism or rights theory – are of little help in the day-to-day ethical decisions which endlessly confront the social worker. I have adopted instead the questions appropriate to a virtue-based ethics and the chapters are organized accordingly. Thus, we shall consider what our relationships ought to be to clients, the agency, the profession, colleagues, and society. What sort of human excellence are we striving for and in what social and political context?

We must begin with the kinds of relationships, institutions, and laws that are our circumstances. If we construct an ethical system that is not grounded in these circumstances, then it will be so remote from our actual lives that we are apt to have no idea how to achieve it.

The ethical systems we have considered are usually set forth as timeless and universal – not tied to particular social and political realities. The differences among the systems, however, suggest the centrality of social and political factors. The Greeks, for example, did not have any concept of "rights" and this was at least in part because the role of Athenian citizens in social and political matters differed from that of eighteenth-century Europeans.

Utilitarianism was in part an eighteenth-century response to the despotism of monarchies and to the accompanying class rigidities and inequities. The notion that every person's happiness was to count equally was a radical, democratic ideal. The first utilitarians were not, however, writing about a society in which large bureaucratic institutions were among the most powerful forces in the society, nor one in which "utility" was reduced to costs and benefits defined in narrow financial terms.

My point is not that we must understand the whole history of our culture before we can make sound ethical judgments, although in fact that is a desirable goal. My point is more limited. To decide among different ethical systems we must consider more than the ethical systems themselves – we must include the social and historical context of which the ethical beliefs are a part.

All of this is important for how we do social work or therapy. To make an informed ethical choice, a worker must develop her own ethical perspective and this must go beyond the ethical to include the political and social beliefs that form an integral part of any vision of how we should live in relation to others. Deciding on "the best course of action" towards a client must be in the context of some understanding of the best sort of society – that is, of the political, economic and social institutions that inevitably affect all our lives.

What this means for us today is that debate about politics and society must be a more explicit part of social work practice. In addition, our ethical deliberations need to go beyond existing ethical frameworks to formulate questions about new social and political realities which the older frameworks did not have to confront. Bureaucratic structures, for example, raise a whole new set of ethical questions which the existing ethical frameworks do not address. The tension between professional and personal ethics also raises new issues for us.

This leads to the questions in the next section. If an ethical system is tied to particular social and political circumstances, won't ethics simply be relative to the culture? Is each of us in the position of choosing our point of view but without any sense that it is more justified than the next? Won't the approach of this book be one more perspective, neither more nor less adequate than any of the others?

I shall argue for a kind of informed relativism or limited objectivity. But first, let us examine relativism more closely.

Relativism

"Relativism" in ethics usually refers to the belief that what a person considers "right" is relative to that person's society or to his or her beliefs, and that there are no compelling reasons to claim that the beliefs or practices of one society or person are better than another's.[21] There is no moral truth other than that of relativism itself.

When we are confronted with belief systems strikingly different from our own, we become unsure how to evaluate them. The temptation seems to be one of two extremes. We may rigidly hold onto our own "moral truths" and try to impose them wholesale on others, or we may conclude that we cannot make any judgments among different moral systems. We must simply accept conflicting judgments as equal in value and conclude that ethics is "relative" or "subjective."

In social work, we seem to have gone from one of these extremes to the other. In the nineteenth-century, social workers were often social missionaries. They imposed their version of "the truth" on reluctant clients whose beliefs we recognize in retrospect as simply being different from those of the workers. Today, as if in reaction to the excesses of the nineteenth century, social workers tend to assume in theory, though not in practice, a professional practice that is "value-free" or unproblematic ethically: the goal of helping is client autonomy, defined as clients' determination of their values and actions. On this model, clients are skillfully guided towards their autonomy, without the imposition of any of the social worker's values. The nineteenth-century ideal is now generally recognized as undesirable. The twentieth-century ideal, however, also is undesirable and needs to be so recognized. It consists either of accepting any and all belief systems as equal in value (different sorts of autonomy), or of imposing one's own values in a subtle way. We seem caught between moralistic fervor and total relativism.

I shall argue that there is a middle course. A limited sort of objectivity is possible, consisting of a constant openness to rationally understanding other points of view and reevaluating one's own in light of them. First, however, we must be clearer about precisely what we are claiming when we claim relativism in ethics. I shall briefly present four versions of relativism, in order to show the misguided nature of each.

(1) Sometimes when we claim relativism in ethics, we are only claiming that there are no broad absolutes applicable to everyone in all circumstances. People ought to keep promises, but it is right for "me" to break a promise under these particular circumstances; therefore, promise-keeping is relative to the circumstances.

This is confusing as an account of relativism, however, because ethics is always relative to the circumstances. If, in this instance, I claim that breaking a promise is the right thing to do, I am usually claiming (a) that keeping promises is in general a good thing, and (b) that in certain circumstances, applicable to everyone, some other ethical factor, like saving a person's life, has more importance. The "ethical truth" here is complex – it cannot be put into one statement that applies to all promises – yet it does not follow that there is no ethical truth. Most ethical systems which claim absolutes like keeping promises or not killing allow for circumstances which appear to violate the principle. Sometimes another principle takes precedence, as when saving a life is more important than keeping a promise. Sometimes the principle is said not really to apply to a situation – as when it is said that killing in self-defense is not really killing. From these qualifications, however, it does not follow that there are no moral truths, only that the truth is complex.

(2) Sometimes the claim that morality is relative or subjective is the claim that we cannot have proven knowledge of moral truths, because our knowledge is limited and fallible. I cannot ever be absolutely certain that breaking this promise is the right thing to do, although I can have strong reasons to believe it is. Because our knowledge is limited, however, it does not follow that there are no moral truths, only that we will never be completely certain what they are.

(3) Sometimes the claim is that ethics is relative to whatever is in "my" interests. This position is described as ethical egoism. Here, however, one is making a definite claim for ethical truth. Ethical truth is whatever is good for me. In determining what is good for me, I am faced with the problems of any ethical theory – what is truly in my interests, as opposed to seeming in my interests? After all, we often make mistakes about what is in our interests. Do my true interests end up excluding the interests of others or including them, and so on? As soon as one brings in these considerations, it becomes harder to show that "good" can be restricted solely to what I want. The attempt, as with the other ethical theories presented, is to discover what truly is good.

(4) Finally, there is real relativism – the belief that there are no moral truths as such. When I claim that an action is "right," this is just a claim about how my culture views "right action" or just my subjective opinion and has no claim to being the truth. I shall show the problems with maintaining this sort of

relativism and shall then argue for a limited kind of objectivity which enables us to be open to others' perspectives.

Total relativism in ethics is as counter-intuitive as is a simple-minded absolutism. To be a complete relativist, one would have to claim that a particular action can be right (for me) but that this carries no more weight than any subjective expression of a preference. I might say, for example, that it is right for me to be honest in most situations but not necessarily right for any other person. What would such a statement mean? It seems I am saying that "I like to be honest" and others like other ways of acting. "Right" amounts to nothing more than a personal preference. But then I will be committed to a position in which nothing is truly better than any other thing – it's just my preference. And this flies in the face of our own experience. We feel quite certain, at least in some extreme cases, that one thing is better than another – for example, that it would have been better if a relative had died without a final year of unrelieved suffering in semi-consciousness. In other situations as well we are convinced that one action must be better than another – that successful completion of a challenging task is better than sadistic teasing of a child. If we change our minds, we do not decide that nothing is better than anything else but rather that we did not know enough and made a wrong judgment about what is truly better. On closer scrutiny, we can and must reject this version of relativism.

The haunting ghost of relativism remains, however, because we are constantly faced with belief systems alien to our own which we do not know how to evaluate. Not just social workers but all of us today are confronted by a confusing array of belief systems – those already mentioned (utilitarianism, rights theories, etc.), as well as those of other cultures and religions – Taoism, Buddhism, cultures in Africa, Asia and elsewhere, and sub-cultures in the United States. On what basis do we decide that some of these, or some of their beliefs, are better than others? If we reject some of the beliefs as harmful, are we simply assuming the superiority of our own belief system in a parochial way? Is the only alternative the indiscriminate acceptance of every belief system? If we are confronted with a different belief system, any judgments we make will seemingly be either from one belief system or another. If we are deciding between utilitarianism and Kantianism or between a Christian viewpoint of middle-American Protestantism and the Islamic beliefs of a poor Black client, what criteria should we use? Won't any criteria be from a particular tradition and therefore relative to that?

I shall argue for what can be viewed as a fifth version of relativism – an *informed relativism* which is historically specific and consistent with a limited sort of objectivity.

"Pure objectivity," seeing reality as it is apart from a point of view, has come to be seen as an impossible goal even in science. We cannot observe anything without in some ways interacting with and thus changing what we observe. Our observations of "the truth" about the object are thus conditioned by the particular observations themselves. In human service work, we must add other complicating factors: we are interacting not with inanimate objects but with people, who in turn respond to our responses to their responses. We are also trying to arrive at truths not just about what is but about what ought to be. Any claim to "objectivity" or "ethical truth" is bound to be limited and qualified.

Thus "objectivity" in ethical decisions always involves having a particular point of view and is always partial. We begin with the belief system, or parts of belief systems, we were taught as children. We reconsider or reject parts of them, when they conflict with interests we develop or with experiences we have. At best, one's point of view takes into account in a rational way as many alternative views as possible.[22]

In addition, in considering competing frameworks, we must consider the problems they were set forth to resolve. Each one has a particular history, and we can only adequately evaluate it if we understand its social and historical context and the purposes it now serves. Utilitarianism was a response to a particular set of problems (including the poverty created by early industrialization) but may serve quite different purposes in our culture today (such as reinforcing a narrow view of utility that increases the burdens of the poor). Ethical systems give direction to our lives in particular social and political circumstances, and those circumstances must be part of our evaluation.

So too, with clients who differ sharply from ourselves, we

need first to understand fully their point of view before we can evaluate it. We need to understand the history and circumstances that gave rise to that point of view and examine whether we have goals in common.

In trying to evaluate a different point of view, we must use all our imagination to enter into that person's way of thinking before making judgments about its adequacy. Too often, we are encouraged to focus serious attention on the psychodynamics of clients but not to take seriously their stand towards the world – including their ethical views – as possibly more adequate than our own. Only if we can do this can we begin to claim objectively.

None of this is easy. It involves a constant reevaluation of one's own position in light of other people's experiences. And, finally, this process is only possible if there are some commonalities to be found among our ethical differences and some common criteria for evaluating different ethical beliefs. There must be some common ground for any sort of objectivity to be possible.

In social work, we assume that our clients and ourselves share the same goals, but this may not always be so. What we mean by goals like "client autonomy" or "social justice" may differ radically, as earlier sections of this chapter show.

I think, however, that we have to assume that there are some commonalities. At least an openness to this possibility may lead to new discoveries about what goals we can construct in common. A basic respect for human dignity, belief in equal opportunity, and desire for community are a sufficient basis for beginning our task of opening new debate about our own and others' points of view. Our objectivity must reside in an openness to reconsider our own perspective on the basis of alternatives that are offered, including those of our clients.

Ethical analysis

Imagination is the quality most often missing in ethical analysis in human service. We must creatively search for new ways of thinking about problems, new arguments, new solutions, as well as entering imaginatively into the client's point of view. Too often we limit our inquiry to an established set of questions or assume constraints imposed by society and therefore limit the possibilities of creative and satisfactory solutions to ethical problems.

Consider again the case of the homeless client, Doris. Whether or not you readmit Doris to the program will depend largely on the sort of relationship you have already established with her and on the beliefs you hold about the agency, other agencies, the homeless, etc. Let us consider again, more systematically, the kinds of questions you should be asking in order to make the best possible decision, and the ways in which you can begin to evaluate the different ethical perspectives introduced earlier.

(1) What is the client's point of view?

As mentioned already, casework focuses on understanding a client, but often such understanding emphasizes clients' psychodynamics and excludes serious consideration of their values or their opinion about how to solve problems. Clients sometimes report that they have never been asked by their workers how they would solve a problem; workers simply assumed that as workers they were in the best position to decide.

In the case of Doris, she should be asked about what she wants and how she views her homelessness. In some cases, clients are unable to answer such questions, but often they can and we can only find this out by asking.

(2) What is my perspective as a worker?

We must have a clear idea of what our goals are – what does it mean to "help" a client? We must have a vision of the sort of society that our work is trying to achieve – what kinds of relationships, economic structure, government regulations, etc. We must be able to justify our perspective and understand its relation to other points of view. Goals in casework are too often construed in narrow terms that leave unexamined their hidden political and social assumptions.

For example, a worker's beliefs about homelessness will clearly affect the way she relates to any particular homeless client, and she needs to understand and be able to justify her view. If she believes that everyone has a right to housing, her actions towards her clients will differ from the person who sees it as a good to be earned, with some temporary relief available for those without any means.

(3) How should I, as a worker, handle differences between my client's and my own views?

Given our pluralistic society, a client may have a different ethical perspective from your own. How you treat these differences will itself involve an ethical stand, and you must be able to justify the position you take. Should you explain your values to the client? Should you attempt to enlist the client as an ally in a common struggle to better conditions for the homeless? Should you try to change clients' beliefs, without informing them that you are doing this?

These questions are basic ones, which a worker needs to examine at the beginning of a casework relationship, as well as when a difficult decision emerges. They will be considered in Chapters 4 and 5.

(4) What choice is required?

Often, the way in which we pose a problem determines the way we solve it. We must first ask whether there really is a problem. If there is, we should consider different ways to view the problem and the ethical and political assumptions involved. Is the problem, for example, whether or not to readmit Doris to the shelter or how to get the shelter expanded? Is Doris's problem one of mental instability or unemployment or simply lack of housing? Is Doris uncooperative or the agency inflexible? We must be aware of the assumptions about larger issues that our problem-solving includes. Chapter 1 illustrated this process of analysis. We should be particularly aware of so-called technical decisions which obscure ethical ones.

(5) What are the alternative courses of action?

This involves gathering data about the situation, evaluating constraints and using one's imagination to think of different alternatives.

In Doris's case, the obvious and immediate alternatives are (a) readmitting her to the shelter or (b) denying her access to it.

Other alternatives include (c) urging the shelter or state to expand services, (d) pressuring the program to take her back, (e) finding her another program or shelter.

(6) What positions do these different alternatives represent and what arguments can be made for each?
Here we encounter quite different levels of complexity. Consider, for example, some of the reasons a worker might give for readmitting Doris to the shelter.

(a) She will suffer if we don't take her back.
(b) She is mentally unstable and needs treatment.
(c) She is mentally unstable and will be a danger or nuisance to the community.
(d) By taking her back, we can pressure the agency and the state to expand services to the homeless.

Each of these reasons includes a mixture of factual and ethical claims which might be disputed. Reason (a) suggests a Kantian perspective, whereas (c) and (d) suggest utilitarian perspectives. Against (c) one might argue that she is not mentally unstable or that the instability is not a social nuisance. One might also argue that even if she is a nuisance, protecting society from her is not an important ethical consideration.

In deciding on a course of action, one must understand the more general ethical position implicit in one's action and its connection to a political and social point of view. If, for example, you put primary importance on Doris's suffering, then what does your attitude towards her reveal? Is your justification a Kantian one, that you must treat her as an end in herself – as deserving respect and placement, regardless of the agency's rules? What more do you assume? Do you view her as a helpless victim of individual circumstances, or the creator of her own misfortune, or a casualty of undesirable economic policies? We might believe that we have a responsibility to help because it is our Christian duty and an act of charity or because Doris has a right to housing (a Marxist or Reamer sort of justification). From a Marxist or rights perspective, we would also believe that we have a responsibility to try to change the economic circumstances that result in homelessness.

Our treatment plans will also reveal ethical and/or political assumptions, as mentioned in Chapter 1. Doris might be placed in a program with structured tasks taught through behavior modification, focused on enabling her to move out into a community residence. Alternatively, she might be placed in a psychiatric program, whose focus is more on providing a supportive environment in which she can act out and resolve issues in her life. While this decision about program will ostensibly be based on Doris's particular needs, it will also reflect the worker's beliefs about the desirability of types of treatment, the role of the professional, and the kind of treatment particular sorts of clients "deserve." These assumptions are often not made explicit, and we will be examining some of them in later chapters.

In deciding what to do, we should seek out those who hold different views from our own. This assures the most open and full discussion of different options.

(7) Is the solution I reach consistent with my goals as a human service worker?

Sometimes we become so focused on the immediate problem and feel so buffeted by pressures from our agency, other agencies, or the community that we lose sight of what we stand for. This question also forces us to clarify for ourselves what our ethical perspective is and whether our current actions are undermining our original goals. If I claim to believe in empowerment but am not taking my clients' views seriously, then I need to reexamine what I am doing.

As social workers, we often face conflicts between what we believe is good for a client and what an agency requires us to do. We must understand the ethical and political assumptions contained in agency policies. Is the policy against readmitting Doris for the benefit of protecting the homeless or simply to make the agency look good? Are appropriate programs bypassed because the agency can more easily get money for other programs? For example, while a state may be willing to allocate some funds for the homeless, it is apt to be more eager to provide funds for the mentally retarded.

We must decide what our responsibility is within such a bureaucray: should we question agency regulations? Should we disobey them when they are unethical? Should we organize other workers, clients, or the public to fight policies? Should we quit? These questions will be considered in Chapter 6.

In subsequent chapters, particular cases will be used to raise some of the most difficult ethical issues confronting social workers in casework – issues of upholding confidentiality, going against a client's wishes, dealing with incompetent co-workers, confronting unethical bureaucratic demands. Answers to the questions posed here will be explored more fully. My hope is that this approach will help social workers evaluate their own ethical perspectives and will result in more debate about political and ethical issues among workers.

3 Violating confidentiality

The Protective Privilege Ends Where the Public Peril Begins.[1]

General issues

The judge didn't really want to send the former nun to jail, but he felt he had no choice. She was adamantly refusing to turn over to the court a file from the rape crisis center where she worked. That file contained information about a fifteen-year-old victim of a rape who'd come in for counseling. The defendant in the rape case wanted the file to prepare his defense, and as the judge . . . interpreted the law, he had a right to it. Thus, when it became clear that Margaret "Peggy" Langhammer, thirty-one, a dropout from the order of the Sisters of Mercy and executive director of the Rhode Island Rape Crisis Center (RCC) would not budge, he ordered her to jail. . . .

Her stay in prison was short: one day. When the victim gave her permission for the file to be released, Langhammer surrendered it to the court and was set free.

It's easy to understand and sympathize with the position Langhammer took. . . . "Part of the healing process after a rape is in just being able to talk about it," Langhammer told The Phoenix in an interview. She added that a victim might not seek a counselor's help if there was a possibility that her most intimate thoughts might one day surface in a courtroom.

Still, it's equally easy to understand why Arthur Donnelly, twenty-five, of North Kingston, Rhode Island, wanted and felt he had a right to the RCC's record of what the fifteen-year-old had said about the assault he was charged with. For all he knew, the RCC file might contain evidence that could allow him to clear his name.[2]

This cases raises fundamental questions about confidentiality. Should social workers always protect the confidences of their clients? Is doing so justified even if it may endanger others or violate their rights? Consider the different kinds of conflicts one may confront.

(1) A teenage client tells you in confidence that she is thinking of committing suicide and does not wish anyone in her family to know.
(2) A co-worker confides in you that she is high on drugs when she works in your day-care center.
(3) You know that your agency is not providing treatment to clients in a day program while telling the public it is doing so.
(4) Your agency is using funds designated for client care to buy expensive furniture for the offices.
(5) Your agency is making client records easily available to anyone in the office, without first informing clients.
(6) Your agency is strict about client confidentiality and will not give out information to other agencies without the proper consent forms. In order to place a client, however, you must give another agency information *today*, without getting the proper forms signed.

Different professions have different public sanctions on confidentiality. Lawyers have been granted almost absolute privilege by the law.[3] Even if a lawyer could prevent harm by revealing a confidence, keeping the confidence is a legal duty, justified by the overall good to society of such trust and privacy. Doctors, too, are obligated not to reveal confidences of patients, with some important exceptions.[4] The exceptions reveal an equally important duty to maintain the welfare of society. In cases of infectious disease or gunshot wounds, for example, a doctor is required to inform appropriate authorities and thus violate the confidentiality of the patient. The clergy claims an equally strong obligation to maintain confidentiality, although the legal sanction has not always been given.[5]

The duty of confidentiality – and its corresponding legal sanction of privileged communication – is less clearly spelled out for most other professionals whom it affects – social workers, journalists, school teachers, insurance agents, nurses, bankers, etc.[6] Many of these groups argue that they have a similar duty to maintain confidentiality, and some – most notably journalists and social workers – have been willing to go to jail rather than reveal a confidence. In considering this issue, we need to look beyond social work to the cumulative effect on society of the privileged communication desired by different professions. While the focus here will be on social work, these broader issues will be part of our consideration.

We will thus be chiefly concerned with two issues, one *moral*, the other *legal*:

(1) Under what conditions ought social workers to maintain confidentiality? What is the social worker's *moral* obligation?
(2) Should there be a legal statute which (a) *enables* or (b) *compels* social workers to protect the confidence of clients?

The moral duty of confidentiality must be distinguished from privileged communication – the explicit legal mandate that social workers need not or must not reveal information entrusted to them. Some states have passed laws giving social workers privileged communication in those cases when clients have explicitly requested it. Even then, certain conditions exempt the social worker from maintaining the confidence, as when criminal proceedings are involved or when the confidence involves the threat of a criminal act.[7] Whatever its legal status, a social worker must still decide whether in any given case maintaining confidentiality is moral; the legal consequences will be part of that deliberation. For example, in Massachusetts, social workers have to report the names of suspected child abusers to the Department of Social Services which has to report them to the District Attorney.[8] In some cases, a social worker may feel that such reporting is wrong, even though *legally* required.

The concept of confidentiality can be clarified by the following two definitions, borrowed from S. Wilson's informative book on confidentiality in social work:

> Confidential information has been defined as those personal facts or conditions pertaining to the client's life which he has communicated to the agency for definite purposes related to the service he is requesting or receiving from the agency.
>
> Confidentiality means that disclosures by the patient or

> client to the professional will not be revealed to others except under certain circumstances and then only for the purpose of helping him.[9]

These definitions include an obligation or duty on the part of social workers to safeguard information entrusted to them by their clients, whether or not the client specifically requests it. The second definition assumes that another obligation may take precedence over confidentiality – the good of the client. We also have to ask whether the overall good of society may require us to break a confidence.

In social work, as in most professions, confidentiality has become complicated by the increased bureacracy of society. Social workers must often keep detailed records that are available to a large number of people – other social workers, administrators, secretaries, and so on. In some mental health facilities, most of the direct service work is done by teams: all the members may know each client's file, without the client being informed. Other agencies also request and need access to these records, and records may be kept rather carelessly for years after a case is closed.[10] Social workers often assume that clients know the extent to which the files are available to other professionals when in fact they do not.

Many violations of confidentiality are the result of convenience, carelessness, or lack of thought. For example, confidential information is not infrequently given over the telephone to an inquiring social worker or doctor or other "professional" whose identity is not verified.[11] The demands of the job are such that social workers can afford little time for obtaining informed consents or for taking extra precautions to assure that records and conversations are kept confidential.

These situations do not, strictly speaking, present ethical dilemmas – there is general agreement that these careless breaches are unethical. They are important because they reveal the increasingly bureaucratic context within which confidentiality must be evaluated. They highlight (1) the kind of almost impossible pressure social workers face, pressure which makes individual ethical decisions seem ineffectual and unimportant; (2) the bureaucratic maze that results in persons being viewed solely as statistics; and (3) a world of massive information-gathering that can result in almost total loss of privacy.

One popular and appealing solution to issues of confidentiality is to "make do" without confronting the basic issues. If records are too easily accessible or if they might be subpoened in court, the solution is to refuse to put anything significant in the record.[12] If a client might reveal criminal activities, then the solution is to avoid asking the client anything about such activities. Unfortunately, this sort of solution is similar to sticking one's head in the sand. The social worker avoids the ethical issue, but since the ethical issue remains, she takes an ethical position by default. If, for example, a client is engaging in criminal activities which harm society in ways that override all other factors, then a social worker is remiss if she does not inquire further when she has suspicions. Similarly, if a court ought to have information from a client interview because of potential harm to society, then a social worker is participating in that harm by in effect "destroying" evidence she has. The evasions described may be appropriate, but only if we can conclude that confidentiality overrides all other claims. First, we must confront the ethical conflicts.

This chapter will focus on the confidentiality between worker and client. Chapter 6 will raise issues of maintaining the confidence of an agency, co-worker, supervisor, or employee, although some of what is discussed here applies to the other situations as well.

A case-study

Consider the following case:

> You are a social worker in a mental health clinic and for two years you have been counseling a thirty-four-year-old woman, Anna, who cannot cope with her sixteen-year-old daughter. The daughter is in treatment with one of your colleagues. You have established a good relationship with Anna, and until recently the mother and daughter have been making progress. Anna is divorced, lives with her daughter in a run-down apartment building, and works as a visiting nurse to private patients. She has low self-esteem and few

friends. Her parents live nearby and she sees them often, though she always fights with them. She finds her daughter increasingly hard to discipline: the daughter sometimes disappears for days at a time and refuses to say where she goes.

At first Anna was suspicious of you; she missed appointments but always returned because of her concern for her daughter. She had difficulty trusting anyone. At the end of two years she began to trust you more, to have a better relationship with her daughter, and to confide details of her personal life. Recently, however, Anna has appeared more agitated, wary, and dishevelled.

Suppose one day you notice that she has been drinking; it is 2:00 p.m. Upon being questioned, Anna says that she sometimes has a few drinks in the morning to calm her nerves. She quickly adds that this book did not interfere with her care of patients.

What ought you to do?

If the case seems unproblematic, then consider these alternatives:

(1) She is not a visiting nurse but a bus driver for school children and she is clearly drinking heavily most of the time.
(2) She is drunk when she sees you and is planning to drive home alone.

The case description is sketchy because the way we choose to describe a case may prejudice the ethical issues. If you focus on Anna's personal history, you may persuade yourself that Anna is "testing" you or that she unconsciously desires your intervention. You may then conclude solely *on the basis of her psychodynamics* that you need to set strong limits or that Anna really wants you to report her. You make a diagnosis of her problem and the diagnosis dictates your response. While this approach may appropriately settle the issue, it is too readily used to evade ethical issues that also require deliberation in their own right. Regardless of Anna's psychodynamics, you must ask what *ethical* justification can be given for maintaining or violating her confidence.

In addition, we must be wary of psychological explanations that posit unconscious needs which are opposed to what Anna says she wants or needs, particularly if it is in our interest for her to have them. It is a presumptuous, if sometimes correct, rationale.[13]

This kind of situation can sometimes be resolved in other ways. You may decide that the danger is negligible or you may be able to persuade Anna to report herself and to quit her job.

Suppose, however, that these solutions do not apply. Suppose further that if you report Anna you are quite convinced that she will cease to trust you and will not continue treatment. She will once again feel betrayed. What ought you to do? How should you think about this case?

Traditional ethical considerations

Bok's account

You want to preserve the trust you have established, to respect Anna's confidence, and to respect her plans for herself. At the same time you want to protect others in society, Anna, and yourself. If some harm should come to one of Anna's patients and you had done nothing, you could be sued. What ethical justifications are relevant in this case? Which ones are most compelling? How do you decide?

This section will begin with Bok's formulation of the relevant ethical principles. Bok, a philosopher, discusses confidentiality in her recent book on secrets.[14] Her discussion, while incomplete, brings out important philosophical questions.

Bok argues that professional confidentiality is justified by four premises:

(1) human autonomy regarding personal information;
(2) respect for relationships;
(3) respect for promises; and
(4) benefit of confidentiality to society and to those in need of advice and aid.

The first three principles are closely related. The first is respect for individuals' privacy. "Without some control over secrecy and openness about themselves, their thoughts and plans, their actions, and in part their property, people could neither maintain privacy nor guard against danger."[15] As Bok and others have pointed out, given the increasingly strong pressures to invade privacy, this principle takes on new importance.

Social workers and other therapists have argued further that without the assurance of privacy, clients will be unwilling to reveal personal matters that are essential to successful therapy.[16] In fact, social workers "invade" privacy through the personal questions they sometimes ask. The social worker serves as an advisor to a private, interior dialogue, which is essential to a person's self-understanding. Encouraging this sort of personal dialogue must be balanced by assurances of privacy.

The second principle is one of respect for relationships. It assumes that relationships can only survive in a viable form if there is a basic trust and respect for shared secrets. Certainly social workers agree that a trusting relationship is essential to casework.[17] Again, by their probing personal questions and by their offers of help, social workers implicitly assume a relationship of trust which they ought then to respect.

Anna's situation dramatically makes this point. One of her problems is that she has been unable to trust anyone. After two years, she has begun to trust the social worker and to reveal some of her personal concerns. If the worker reports her, she will (1) violate the privacy that Anna takes for granted and (2) break the trust that seems essential to changing Anna's outlook.

The third related principle is that of respect for promises. If confidentiality has been promised, then to break it is to break one's contract. We have an obligation to keep our promises. Even if an explicit promise has not been made, the presumption of trust and privacy strongly suggests an implicit promise to respect confidentiality. The first three principles resemble a Kantian justification of confidentiality, with focus on the respect and dignity owed to every individual.

The fourth principle justifies professional confidentiality on the basis of its usefulness to individuals and society – a utilitarian justification. Even if it results in harm in some cases, its overall good outweighs such harm. The overall good in social work will be the support and therapy social workers offer, goods which would not be obtainable, or would be severely restricted, without the assurance of confidentiality. Applying this principle to Anna's case, although her alcoholism may endanger others, her worker should maintain confidentiality, because it makes possible help and support, not only to Anna but to many others in society who seek the help of social workers.

Bok argues, I think correctly, that while these principles give strong reasons for upholding confidentiality, there is another, even more important principle – that of protecting society. If keeping a confidence will result in harm to innocent persons, we are not justified in keeping it. The principle of protecting society must be part of the discussion, and in some cases it will outweigh the other four principles. Autonomy over information and respect for privacy should not extend to plans of violence and harm. Further, while a trusting relationship with the social worker is desirable, that good does not justify risking harm to another person. This is particularly compelling, says Bok, as no one has established (1) that confidentiality is essential to effective therapy or (2) that restricting confidentiality decreases the benefits of therapy.[18]

How are we to apply what Bok says to Anna's case and other similar ones? If you report Anna's alcoholism, you may destroy the relationship and further reinforce Anna's distrust of people and her feelings of betrayal. If, however, you believe that significant harm could befall the patients she cares for, then you should warn Anna's employer or persuade Anna to quit her job. The potential harm will take precedence over the relationship.

While Bok's analysis is helpful, there are two key problems: (1) her analysis is too general to provide much guidance for deciding cases; the principles she presents need to be more clearly connected to a larger social/political outlook. (2) She needs to address the inequality inherent in professional relationships of confidentiality. Paradoxical as it sounds, her account is neither general nor specific enough.

As fundamental to her moral picture, Bok mentions both belief in human life as having the highest worth and belief in our responsibility to lighten "the collective burden of suffering, ignorance, and evil in human lives."[19] Bok does not specify further the ethical/social/political context of her five principles. She presents them without telling us what others are relevant. Having a more complete social and political outlook would help precisely because the social worker could then give further content to the five principles. We need to know more about what counts as a desirable society in order to know what counts as autonomy or trust or significant harm, and thus what sort of confidence-making to engage in.

Of particular relevance, professional confidentiality assumes a relationship of expertise and one-sided revelations. Bok never discusses the inequality inherent in such relationships or the inequalities inherent in most "helping" relationships. To evaluate it adequately, we must have thought about the sorts of personal relationships a society should foster and the consistency of these ideals with our existing practices. A socialist perspective, with its emphasis on breaking down class divisions, would lead a social worker to be wary of professional confidentiality, with its one-sidedness and assumption of expertise. By not focusing more on the relationship itself – and the dangers of its power, Bok leaves unquestioned basic issues about the value of professional relationships and their role in possibly reinforcing client helplessness. This broader issue will be taken up in the next section, "Issues of power."

Bok leaves us with the worth of the individual but no sense of what social and political arrangements would promote that worth or would justify her position on confidentiality. If she provided this basis, it might give further guidance in applying her five principles to particular cases.

If we apply the ethical perspectives described in Chapter 2 to Anna's case, we will see that they are of even more limited value. Cases involving confidentiality are sometimes posed as particularly dramatic examples of the confiict between Kantian and utilitarian ethics.[20] Kantianism seemingly favors keeping confidences at any cost in order to preserve the respect owed to the client. It focuses on the first three of Bok's principles: (1) autonomy over personal information; (2) respect for the relationship; and (3) respect for promise-keeping. Utilitarianism, on the other hand, favors breaking confidences if doing so will result in the greatest amount of good. It focuses on Bok's fourth and fifth principles: (4) the usefulness to society of maintaining confidences; and (5) the good of protecting society, even if that involves breaking a confidence. One must calculate where the greatest good lies.

In Anna's case, as in the case of the homeless client, each perspective can be used to justify opposite courses of action. On one interpretation of the Kantian view, one should preserve the confidence, seemingly even if great harm would result, for example, if Anna were a bus driver or airline pilot. On another interpretation of Kant, however, keeping the confidence would violate the respect owed to others involved, their very lives. It might also violate the respect owed to Anna in forcing her to accept responsibility for the consequences of her actions. Our moral intuitions in the extreme cases will result in our reinterpreting the Kantian principle or throwing it out.[21]

Similarly, we can use utilitarianism to justify keeping the confidence (the general good to society of maintaining confidences) or breaking it (the harm to society in this case).[22]

Applying the rights-based theories can also result in opposite resolutions of the case: we can argue for the client's right to privacy and right to confide her problems to someone in order to sort them out, and we can argue for the rights of others in society to be protected from her drunkenness. To decide what to do, we must work out which rights are most important and what sort of society they presuppose.

All of these perspectives have in common basic elements that have structured a great deal of ethical discussion and yet which seem to contribute to their inadequacy. Each claims to provide an impartial, universal set of criteria for determining what is moral. Each focuses on individual action – on the autonomous individual's rational deliberations, apart from any particular community, social setting, or historical context. Yet these assumptions do not seem appropriate to the kinds of situations social workers face. The model may only fit situations dreamed up by philosophers – and too often this sort of example is given.

Social workers, however, make decisions about people over whom they usually have considerable power. The model of a world of autonomous individuals is misleading. The nature of the institutions within which the social worker operates – usually large-scale bureaucratic organizations in which neither worker nor client is autonomous – is central to making an informed decision. Any theory that leaves this out or abstracts completely from it is likely to be of limited value. The rest of this chapter will consist of an attempt to explore some of the neglected features which form a central place in social life, in social work decisions and thus also in ethics. These features include the nature of the relationship between worker and client and the power inherent in it. My comments will draw on aspects of Marxist critiques of social work practice.

Issues of power

Bok, in talking about secrecy, imagines four hypothetical societies which reflect different arrangements of secrecy.[23] The first is one in which you and I cannot keep anything secret, but others can. "We are transparent to them, either because we are incapable of concealment or because they have means of penetrating all our defenses." The second society is the reverse of the first. You and I can pierce the secrets of others, but they cannot pierce ours. Bok suggests that neither of these two societies would be desirable. Their contrast reveals clearly how much power resides in knowing secrets, particularly if it is not reciprocal.

More disturbing, the two societies resemble the relationship between social worker and client to an uncomfortable extent. Confidentiality in casework is almost always one-sided. The social worker encourages the client to reveal personal matters and is taught not to reveal anything about her own personal life and little about her personal opinions. Usually the social worker has other kinds of power over the client as well – the power to give money, take away children, combat bureaucracies – power conferred on her by her agency. And there are often class or racial differences, which may increase the client's sense of powerlessness.[24]

These inequalities have not been given the central place they warrant in discussions of confidentiality and of its ethical basis. In both Kantian and utilitarian ethics, the model is of rational individuals acting autonomously in the world. Contemporary ethical theories – such as by Rawls or Gewirth – structure moral principles so that no one person or group will acquire disproportionate power, but they do not focus on how existing power differences affect individual decisions we make on issues like confidentiality. Even Bok, who in her discussion mentions the vulnerability of those seeking help, says little about the effects of radical inequalities on confidentiality. Her examples tend to be drawn from psychiatry and law, professions which deal much less than social work with poor people and class differences.

Discussions in social work, however, also tend to ignore these inequalities. Social workers consider clients' particular circumstances, including their unequal status, important in helping, but not in understanding the *ethical* issue of confidentiality.

The rest of this section describes the central role inequality plays in questions of confidentiality. To understand its significance, we must explore the client's point of view as well as the social worker's, thereby making more precise the differences in outlook. These differences will then enable us to reexamine confidentiality in light of what we find.

The relatively few studies of clients' assessments of social services reveal that they often have a different view of "treatment" from social workers.[25] In research reported in *The Client Speaks*, for example, Mayer and Timms report that while social workers had quite definite norms about the nature of the professional-client relationship, "clients were not always aware of these norms; or if they were aware of them . . . they did not always accept them."[26]

Some of these norms were (1) that the professional keep personal feelings from interfering with treatment; (2) probe intimate aspects of the client's life; (3) guarantee confidentiality; and (4) limit the interaction to the professional relationship, rather than a friendship. Clients, however, often felt (1) that the social worker was not emotionally neutral and was in some cases punitive or indifferent; (2) that the worker had no right to ask personal questions; (3) that confidentiality was not assured; and (4) that the interaction, if successful, was one of friendship.[27] These differences, as well as others, also often characterized the relationships between white social workers and minority clients.[28] Timms argues that social workers need to understand these differences in expectation and to "resocialize" clients to professional norms.[29]

The clients' assumptions may derive, however, from a realistic appraisal of the differences between worker and client. Many of these clients seem to recognize the power the social worker has and the ways it can affect "helping" and "trust." In the study, interviews were often seen as cross-examinations where the client had to figure out and give the right answers and make the right impression. One woman describes the way her mother would help her decide what to say to the social worker:

> I used to go to my mum's because I had left the boy with her and I told mum what I said to the gentleman. And she used to just sit there, saying, "well that was right" or "that was wrong." Or, "you shouldn't have said that – you should have said this". . . . Whatever I said wrong, my mum used to put right. And if the subject came up again the next time I went to the FWA [Family Welfare Association], I knew what to say and would tell it the right way. I used to improve myself each time by my mum talking to me . . .[30]

Not enough studies have been done to draw reliable conclusions about clients' perceptions of casework. Consider, however, what casework must look like from at least some clients' point of view. Take, again, the "case of Anna."

> As Anna, you are a thirty-four-year-old woman who is struggling to support yourself and your daughter. You have always felt that your life is barely under your control, and you are frightened that your daughter will leave or shame you. You feel that somehow you always end up doing things wrong. Your parents blame you for your daughter's problems, and now the school has told you that you have to see a social worker. Well, you'd better do as they say. So you go to see the social worker, and she seems nice enough. She is about ten years older than you and is expensively dressed. Clearly she has lots of education and must make plenty of money; she seems very much in control. You cannot imagine that you and she have anything in common, but she seems

> friendly and you don't really have much choice. After all, what she tells your daughter will carry a lot more weight than anything you have to say. She says that she is there to help you . . . that you should trust her. . . .

In this sort of situation, regardless of other circumstances, trust will not come easily. The client feels desperate and knows that the social worker is in a position to do something – to help or perhaps to make matters worse. It hardly seems surprising that clients would interpret interviews as "cross-examinations" and would be wary of the social worker.

Let us take the case further.

> For two years you go to see this social worker, Miss Smith. You watch her carefully. She seems to understand what you tell her and she seems to care. She gives you some good suggestions about your daughter and you feel better. You begin to tell her more. Your job becomes more demanding and suddenly you feel that too many demands are being made of you. You start drinking. You feel desperate. You have to talk to someone.
>
> Maybe you can talk to Miss Smith. She said to trust her.

Suppose that Miss Smith – following Bok's guidelines – decides that Anna's actions are dangerous to others; she informs Anna of her decision to break the confidence. In this situation, Anna may be justified in feeling betrayed and wronged. If Miss Smith was not explicit about the limits of confidentiality, she will have encouraged Anna in a misleading way to be open and trusting. She will have said that she wanted to help and that she was to be trusted; without further clarification this strongly suggests an implicit promise of confidentiality.

One basic problem in this and other dilemmas of confidentiality is that the nature of the relationship was not adequately spelled out at the beginning nor redefined as it changed. To be asked to "trust" and to talk openly to a stranger who has power over your life is an odd situation, and studies by Timms and others indicate that many clients indeed find it odd. Some resent the personal questions and only answer when pushed continually to do so. "You're not entitled to ask people questions like that, are you really? Well, I don't think you are. . . ."[31] Some clients assumed that workers asked personal questions because they were nosey, interested in gossip or trying to annoy. And clients were often unfamiliar with professional norms of confidentiality.[32] When clients' and workers' expectations are so different, misunderstandings and distrust are to be expected. As Timms puts it:

> There is almost a Kafkaesque quality about these worker-client interactions. To exaggerate only slightly, each of the parties assumed that the other shared certain of his underlying conceptions about behavior and the ways in which it might be altered. Then, unaware of the inappropriateness of his extrapolations, each found special reasons to account for the other's conduct.[33]

Establishing a contract with a client is standard practice in casework. Workers usually focus, however, on the goals of treatment. They may not clarify basic assumptions about the relationship itself. Sometimes the question of confidentiality is not even brought up at the beginning of treatment, and when it is, it is often done in a perfunctory way. This is not surprising. After all, it is awkward for a social worker or any therapist who is attempting to establish rapport to begin with a discussion of the conditions under which information will and will not be kept confidential. Without some such discussion, though, a client will not know what to expect. The client may well feel like someone in the hypothetical society Bok describes – transparent to the worker, probed by her, without any way of equalizing the relationship or even of understanding its limits.

It is my belief that some sort of explicit contract about confidentiality should be made with each client. The limits of that contract will vary with the ethical and political beliefs of social worker and client. There will be other limits as well: (1) the legal limits of confidentiality; (2) limits imposed by the goals of the agency; (3) limits derived from the canons of the profession, and so on. For example, a social worker employed by the school department may set different limits to confidentiality with Anna than Miss Smith, because of the different constraints and goals of their agencies, even if they agree on the goals of treatment.

Making an explicit contract of this sort may seem impossibly awkward and counter-therapeutic, as well as time-consuming. One might argue that it will make clients more distrustful and less willing to talk. It will not put them at ease and may frighten them. Besides, a social worker cannot cover every kind of confidential information that might come up.

Some sort of explicit discussion, however, is essential; (1) It is morally obligatory because a client should know precisely what is being promised, and only in doing so can we build towards a client's autonomy. And (2) it may be beneficial pragmatically as well, both to clients and workers. It may, for example, be reassuring to clients who do not know what to expect. It can serve to educate clients about the nature of the relationship and its goals, and it gives them more control over the situation, by defining more precisely the ways in which their confidences may be used. In addition, while explicit contract-making will not resolve all difficult cases of confidentiality, it will help the social worker to clarify her position to herself and her clients before, rather than after, facing hard choices. The clarification should include (1) the specific ways in which confidences will be honored or may be violated or (2) at least basic guidelines about confidence-keeping. For example, these might include rules about reporting child abuse, felonies, or misuse of welfare funds, as well as rules about routine disclosure of information to a supervisor or at staff meetings.

Positions on confidentiality

This section provides some examples of how the social worker's ethical and political assumptions affect her view of confidentiality. The positions presented are not the only relevant ones, but they illustrate the ways in which our actions on confidentiality combine ethical, political, and psychological perspectives.

The American Psychiatric Association, and many social workers as well, take the stand that the relationship between therapist and client should be confidential except in situations of extreme danger to others.[34] The position is based in part on acceptance of a neo-Freudian view of person, society, and individual change.[35] This view contains at least two different sorts of political and ethical assumptions: (a) those about human nature, society, and the goals of treatment; and (b) those inherent to the relationship defined between therapist and client.

Engelhardt succinctly describes the way in which psychotherapy of this sort defines an individual's values; "the healthy, 'normal man' comes to grips (a) with his inner impulses and (b) with outer reality considered generally. A certain personal autonomy or personal integrity is embraced as a *summum bonum*. Psychotherapy is engaged in augmenting the autonomy of the self."[36] Individual autonomy is the goal and it is achieved by coming to grips with inner impulses and external reality. This, however, requires personal revelations of repressed fears and fantasies, revelations which will only be forthcoming in a relationship of trust to a skilled therapist. Thus, confidentiality is essential to the success of this sort of therapy.

Psychotherapy, however, while it commits a therapist to confidentiality, is consistent with quite different political and ethical outlooks, which in turn provide different limits to confidentiality. The goal of psychotherapy – most generally stated as mental health or social functioning or autonomy – may be defined as helping individuals function well within the existing society or helping to liberate them from repressive social institutions.[37] It thus lends itself both to status quo and reformist political beliefs. These assumptions are relevant to confidentiality, since it will be maintained except in situations of danger to others. What counts as endangering others will depend upon more general assumptions about society. For example, if you tell Anna that you cannot maintain confidentiality in situations in which others are endangered, you should give Anna some idea of what *you* count as danger. Suppose that you have to decide whether or not to tell Anna's daughter, against Anna's wishes, that Anna is dying of cancer. Does the confidence endanger the daughter's well-being? Your view will depend in part on your beliefs about family and its relation to society. If you believe that parents should have full jurisdiction over their children in order to preserve the family, your view will differ from the social worker who believes strongly in children's rights.

Thus, while psychotherapy commits a social worker to belief in individual autonomy and in confidentiality, the goals of treatment can be formulated consistent with different political outlooks and thus also with different limits to confidentiality. A therapist, then, should make clear to the client the underlying basis of her concept of confidentiality.

The *process* of psychotherapy also places limits on confidentiality. Therapy's focus – individual, family, group – will determine the primary allegiance of the therapist and thus the primary relationship of confidentiality.

In addition, the egalitarian or authoritarian nature of the relationship will affect the limits one puts on confidentiality. Traditional psychiatric psychotherapy places a strong emphasis on transference and on unconscious determinants of behavior. Clients are encouraged to recreate their early attachments through the relationship to the therapist. Thus, clients' expressed wants must be reinterpreted through the therapist's more detached eye, and they are encouraged to become dependent in order to understand better and thus to resolve their personal problems.[38]

A therapist engaging in this sort of therapy is choosing an authoritarian process, in which she extends power over the client, because of her expertise and the encouraged dependency. This results in a one-sided confidentiality.[39] The built-in inequality may be particularly significant when combined with other inequalities such as race, class, etc. It is an inequality that is easily abused – it can lead to perpetuating dependency, to ignoring clients' demands, or to unjust manipulation of clients.

The social worker should evaluate whether this sort of psychiatric casework and its accompanying confidentiality are consistent with her other beliefs. It is consistent with our existing social arrangements in which expertise and hierarchy figure importantly, but is difficult to make consistent with a socialist perspective, for example. Socialist social workers are committed to breaking down this kind of authoritarian process between social worker and client.

Whatever the particular solution, the therapeutic process itself commits a social worker to beliefs which in turn shape the limits of confidentiality. Confidentiality must be examined in terms of all the relevant beliefs – beliefs underlying both the goals and process of therapy, the client's beliefs, and so on.

Let us turn again to a case and examine how different positions on confidentiality reflect different assumptions.

> You are counseling Anna, who cannot cope with her sixteen-year-old daughter. (See page 61 for details of the case.) Anna tells you that she is dying of cancer but does not want her daughter or the social worker seeing her daughter to know. You cannot persuade her that this is an unwise decision.
>
> What should you do?

Your decision will depend on many factors not adequately elaborated here – on Anna's capacity to choose rationally, on her reaons for not telling her daughter, on the nature of your relationship. Your focus will be on negotiating with Anna and figuring out her motivation for this secret. You may feel tempted to make a decision solely on the various psychodynamic and environmental factors involved and not to evaluate the political and ethical factors. Your decision, however, will also reflect ethical and political assumptions, implicitly if not explicitly.

(1) Suppose you respect Anna's confidence. You may do so because you believe you must preserve the relationship and help Anna with this crisis. You may believe that Anna is in the process of working through her transference to you. You will then be committed to a view in which the rights of the daughter do not figure prominently and in which individual privacy and trust are more important than the relationship between family members or the potential harm to the daughter.

(2) The N.A.S.W. Code of Ethics would require that you tell the other social worker. If the social worker is told but the daughter is not, this commits you to a view of the primacy of the professional relationship and an allegiance to your colleagues and the profession over the expressed interests of the client.

(3) Suppose that you do not honor the confidence and you tell the daughter about the cancer. You may assume that the daughter has a right to know, because children have certain rights in relation to their parents. In this case, your view about

children's rights or the general welfare may take precedence over the relationship to Anna. Your action may reflect a belief that Anna will come to see the wisdom of her daughter knowing. Here you put strong emphasis on your professional expertise and must carefully consider whether it serves to mask personal preferences of your own.

(4) You may assume that only by telling the daughter the truth can the family unit be preserved. Truthfulness will foster trust within the family, and families are essential to preserving our traditional virtues of family loyalty and respect.

The contrasts in these positions indicate that the differences in point of view may be subtle and unacknowledged. What is more, they cannot be settled by knowing the psychodynamics of the case. They reveal different ethical points of view which may entail different limits to confidentiality. The second, third, and fourth positions are all consistent with the principles listed in the N.A.S.W. Code of Ethics, so the Code does not provide guidance in making the choice. What is required along with discussion of relevant casework principles is discussion of the hidden agenda – assumptions about the nature of the family, of social goals, of the role of professionalism.

Consider another situation.

> Again you are counseling Anna, who cannot cope with her sixteen-year-old daughter. Anna tells you that she lied to your agency about her income so she would receive more benefits.
>
> What ought you to do?

In this situation, your decision will depend on the nature of the agency and your beliefs about how it ought to function, as well as on other factors already mentioned. If, for example, you work for a state and federally-funded public welfare department, you may have little contact with any one client and no real relationship to the client, nor any assumption of trust. Further, your clients will be poor people in need of basic services, as opposed to working- or middle-class people with a few more resources. You may decide not to report Anna because of her desperate need, whereas you would report the lying of middle-class clients in a private agency. Either way, your decision will be influenced by your personal beliefs about your responsibilities to the agency (and society) and to the client. Consider a few possible resolutions and the assumptions they make.

Suppose the agency is the public welfare department.

(1) You respect the confidence because you believe that all people have a right to basic services and that the agency does not provide adequately. You believe your foremost responsibility is to the client.
(2) You report the client because you believe that your duty is to carry out the regulations of the agency. You may believe that only in this way can you be just towards all clients, even though you disagree with the agency's restrictive policies towards financial aid and believe them to be counter to the clients' interests.
(3) On the other hand, you may report the client because you believe that the state is already giving out too many benefits and that these clients are undermining the free enterprise system.

The political assumptions need to be spelled out further, but enough has been said to make the point. In this kind of situation, the client's interests may conflict with those of the agency and of society. Your determination of the "real interests" of each and the appropriate limits to confidentiality will inevitably be shaped by your own political beliefs.

Whatever your stand, if you believe in empowering clients, then you should talk to clients about confidentiality from the start. Clients do not expect to be able to trust workers in these situations, but they needn't feel bewildered by mixed messages, which foster distrust on both sides. Workers become known informally as "good" or "punitive" workers, and this often designates workers' implicit assumptions. Making the assumptions explicit can serve to dignify the relationship, as well as to show respect for the client. Without such clarification, professional confidentiality in social work practice can become a bad joke, a way of manipulating and bewildering clients, rather than empowering them.

Professional confidentiality poses special problems for socialist social workers because socialists are committed to breaking down divisions of hierarchy and inequality between worker and client. Several solutions are possible. (1) Workers may discourage confidences from clients and instead encourage clients to organize self-help groups, which could include sharing of confidential information. (2) Workers may attempt to make confidentiality mutual, by sharing with clients information about themselves. This solution, however, may involve breaking professional norms of appropriate behavior by introducing personal views (see Code of Ethics 1.A.1 and 11A1 3).[40] (3) Workers may decide to maintain one-sided confidentiality and educate clients about the political and ethical assumptions implicit in casework situations.

Recommendations

(1) *Making an explicit contract with clients*
To make informed decisions about confidentiality, social workers should think in more specific and also more general terms, paradoxical as that sounds. Social workers should make explicit contracts about confidentiality with each client. Only if we do so are we acting so as to empower our clients. A contract should indicate the limits of confidentiality imposed by society, the agency, the profession, the clients, and the social worker's own outlook. Actual discussion of some sort ought to take place, since only in this way can the social worker have any assurance that the client understands the limits of confidentiality.

A chart can summarize the kinds of constraints on confidentiality that both social worker and client should recognize.

LIMITS ON CONFIDENTIALITY
(1) Law (State and Federal Statutes)
(2) Agency (rules and regulations)
(3) Psychological Model
  Goals of Treatment (view of society, family, social change, and thus of harm and benefit)
 Process of Treatment
  selection of primary client
  authoritarian vs. egalitarian relationship
  nature of professionalism

(4) Beliefs of client
(5) Personal beliefs of social worker

The extent to which a worker spells these out will depend on many factors, such as the nature of the agency and the kind of service involved. The image of a worker sitting down with a severely depressed and unstable client and launching into a description of her political beliefs is clearly ridiculous and would be insensitive. This should not lead us to conclude, however, that such discussion is never appropriate. If we are serious about helping clients and establishing respectful relationships with them, then they should know something about the beliefs we hold that may affect them.

An explicit contract about confidentiality should be made whenever possible, and preferably early in the relationship. A short hand-out explaining the nature and limits of confidentiality can make such discussion easier. Agencies should be encouraged to develop this sort of brochure, and to review it periodically. This can serve to educate both clients and workers and provide a continuing forum for keeping the issues alive.

A worker cannot know for certain whether a client understands the limits of confidentiality – some clients may not hear whatever you say. That is not, however, reason to ignore the issue. Too often we assume that clients will not understand or already do understand when in fact they would welcome such a discussion. When a worker has considerable power over a client's life the limits need to be all the more carefully described.

(2) Understanding your own belief system

In addition to such specific contracts, each social worker should be clear, at least to herself, what her general ethical and political outlook is. Her outlook is not remote from decisions about confidentiality; in fact, it partially determines them. Depending on her beliefs, the social worker may choose to encourage or discourage confidentiality. A social worker who accepts Reamer's ethical framework will encourage confidentiality, with some qualifications, whereas a socialist may discourage it altogether, because of the inequality it fosters. Social workers should consider whether confidentiality itself should be eliminated, but such discussion can only take place if we recognize that there are competing views within social work and that confidentiality itself raises ethical questions.

(3) Treating confidentiality with caution
Because the professional relationship imposes an inequality between therapist and client, confidentiality should be treated cautiously. It attempts to establish "trust" in a situation of unequal power, without any real checks on that power. If therapist and client have equal status outside of that relationship – as is more often the case with social workers and clients in private practice – the confidentiality may not be damaging. If therapist and client are of very unequal status, then the danger is that the power can be too easily misused and that the trust is not freely given because of a coercive element to the relationship. Perhaps only a very limited "trust" is desirable in such circumstances. We should constantly ask ourselves whether confidentiality will help to empower, or undermine empowerment, of the client.

(4) Making the agency more responsible about confidentiality
One of the most important factors in decisions about confidentiality is having the time to think about it and *recognizing it as an ethical issue.* Periodic staff meetings which focus on confidentiality should be a standard part of social work practice and should include discussion of political assumptions, as well as specific contracts.

In addition, agencies should always have an *outside* consultant who advises on difficult cases. Being outside the agency, the consultant would be free of the particular concerns which can bias those in the agency. For example, a case conference about Anna might put undue emphasis on the danger to the agency of being sued without giving adequate attention to other equally relevant factors.

Agencies violate confidentiality most often through careless handling of case records. Strict procedures on record-keeping should be implemented to protect client-confidentiality, and there should be regular reviews both of the procedures and of staff's awareness of them. Even when we have good procedures, there is a tendency to ignore or bypass them, so regular reminders are essential. Focusing on confidentiality can be one way to combat the natural tendency of any bureaucratic organization to slide into disrespect of the client.

(5) Establishing professional guidelines

Finally, there are the questions raised at the beginning of the chapter. Should social workers establish professional guidelines on confidentiality? Should they press for legal protection?

While social work as a profession should require workers to make explicit contracts with every client on the limits of confidentiality, it should not establish any one position. (1) Different agency settings require such different limits on confidentiality that one set of guidelines would be inappropriate or misleading. (2) In addition, social workers hold quite different ethical and political beliefs, which result in different positions on confidentiality. The profession should encourage debate about these different beliefs. Such debate would enrich social work and help to clarify differences in the profession.

(6) Establishing a legal sanction

If these are the professional guidelines for confidentiality, then should social workers have any legal protection? The case at the beginning of the chapter describes a social worker forced either to violate the confidence of a client in a rape crisis center or to go to jail. Shouldn't some sort of privileged communication be given?

This question is the most difficult to answer. As Bok and Wilson point out, we do not know enough about the effects of confidentiality – its necessity in treatment or the harm it produces. In addition, as mentioned early in the chapter, the legal sanction for social work should be in the context of legal sanctions for other professions. At the moment, doctors, lawyers, counselors, school personnel, clergy, and social workers all have or want privileged communication, and most give somewhat similar rationales for wanting it. If they all receive it, we will have a society in which an increasing number of people are freed in important ways from the obligation to tell when they know of immoral action. It is dangerous ever to exclude any person from the obligation to inform others of significant immoral action. It relieves a person from having to think in moral terms about a whole range of actions or persons and this in turn encourages an amoral stance. If most professionals are thus relieved of thinking about ethics in many of their professional interactions to clients, then the effect on society may be of an increasingly amoral outlook by both professionals and clients. So far, only lawyers have that exclusive privilege, and it is not at all clear from the current practices of lawyers that this has been beneficial to society.

The dangers of privileged communication can be put another way. If it is given to social workers, an obligation to respect confidentiality may be created. Thus, if Anna tells Miss Smith that she (Anna) is an alcoholic but also a visiting nurse (or teacher or airline pilot), Miss Smith would be obligated not to do anything about it. Thus, indirectly, she would be responsible *in moral terms* (though not legally) if harm resulted from Anna's condition. In spite of all the ethical dilemmas a social worker now faces, that worker may be better off juggling the obligation to client with that to society, rather than being obligated to make decisions that are sometimes quite clearly unethical.

Some sort of more limited legal sanction, however, may well be appropriate for social work – and other professions as well. It would protect the client from arbitrary revelations of confidences by the social worker and would provide the basis for some sort of limited trust and help. The limits of that confidentiality, however, should be decided on the basis of the extensive public debate which is now beginning to emerge, and it must take into account general social and political goals of which the issue of confidentiality forms only one small part.

4 Influencing the client: whose values are promoted?

It is the counselor's vocation to change people's opinion about themselves and about the world.[1]

The most effective stance in the quest for power is the one that appears least political.[2]

The moral dimension of language

Counseling of some sort is at the heart of social work practice.[3] It is often what makes onerous administrative tasks and endless paper work bearable. It gives form to social workers' central task: to help others.

Although "counseling" is sometimes distinguished from "therapy" as more directive, with focus on specific time-limited goals such as resolving marital conflicts or evaluating a pregnancy, I shall use the term more generally to mean helping a person through conversation.

Whatever its form, counseling in social work is an attempt to change others in some way – to increase their autonomy, to enable them to love and to work, to make the world better – and in this sense it is "moral reeducation." No matter how nondirective the therapeutic form, a social worker

> is guided by a belief system – by some vision of the kind of changes that would improve his patient's life. He is also guided by some moral principle that limits the extent to which he would help a patient obtain happiness at the expense of the happiness of others.[4]

At root, counseling involves the modification of values.

We must ask, then, *what values should inform counseling or therapy?* How should a therapist act so as not to impose values on clients, yet also so as to prevent clients from acting in destructive ways.

I shall argue that these issues are usually discussed in a misleading way. While therapists acknowledge that value considerations are always a part of their work, nonetheless they discuss therapy as if it were somehow politically and ethically neutral. Goals, like autonomy, love, work, and self-actualization, are assumed to make ethical and political commitments which are universally accepted.[5] They are distinguished from more specific and controversial judgments on topics like abortion, nuclear war, or employment, about which therapists are taught to remain neutral. On this view, a therapist should urge a client not to commit suicide, but should neutrally inquire about the client's reasons for having an abortion. Halmos takes this position when he acknowledges the key role of the therapist's values and then goes on to urge "a non-involved involvement" or "keenly interested neutrality."[6] The ideal of the interested-but-detached, neutral therapist persists.

This chapter will focus primarily on therapeutic practices in psychiatric casework, in order to examine the ethical dilemmas inherent in even this seemingly neutral kind of counseling. I will present five cases in order to make two kinds of points. (1) Any therapeutic position, even that of Szasz's autonomous psychoanalysis, makes specific ethical and political commitments.[7] These commitments have sometimes been inadequately recognized because discussion has not been sufficiently rooted in concrete cases.[8] The choice is not whether or when you bring values into therapy; my point is that you cannot help bringing them in. (2) The choice, then, is: what values, what ethical and political points of view, should you present to the client? Responses to the cases will be examined in order to reveal the different sorts of commitments presupposed, and to compare alternatives.

Before turning to the cases, however, some comments must be made about language, and its moral dimensions. Because our language and thoughts are intertwined, they may reinforce each other in dangerous ways: we know that our descriptions of clients affect our view of them, and we can all too easily slip into ways of talking that obscure the judgments we make. Consider, for example, the following social work questions.

(1) Who needs treatment? What needs treatment?

(2) What is a successful outcome of treatment?
(3) How can we best achieve this outcome?

Because the questions are directed to "the experts," the professionals, as those truly qualified to answer them, they are apt to discourage us from taking the client seriously as an equal partner in decision-making.

> When the capacity to define the problem becomes a professional prerogative, citizens no longer exist. The prerogative removes the citizen as problem-definer, much less problem-solver. It translates political functions into technical and technological problems.[9]

The concepts themselves disguise from us our moral and political judgments. "Need," for example, suggests a deficiency within the client, rather than a right or a condition to be met.[10] It suggests an objective, biologically-based criterion, such as food or shelter. Human needs, however, are more complex than food and shelter and are indistinguishable from human wants and interests. We might disagree, for example, about whether spirituality is a basic human need. To decide what "needs" are "basic" is in effect to decide what human activities and desires are most important.[11] In talking of "needs," then, we posit values, but without making them explicit.

The use of medical terminology is apt to reinforce a view of the client as passive and of problem-solving as value-free. "Illness," "symptom," "diagnosis," "treatment," and diagnostic categories all suggest empirically verifiable, objective malfunctions of an organic sort. As many critics have pointed out, however, most people who receive social services do not have malfunctions which are known to be biologically-based.[12] Even with established mental disorders, many do not fit the medical model. They are selected on the basis of the unhappiness they cause the client or the social malfunctioning they entail, not on the basis of "medical need." We, as social workers, not scientists, decide what counts as a social malfunction and which malfunctions are most serious. Thus, if we "diagnose" a client as having a "borderline personality," we are making (and accepting) judgments about how people *should* function and what their lives *should* be like. When people's problems are described as medical phenomena, however, we may overlook the value judgments we make.

By contrast, goals of treatment are often described in general, euphemistic language which is also misleading. Intimacy, self-actualization, integrity, identity are often described as if they were "natural" stages of any person's development, rather than particular values.[13] The goal of autonomy, or self-determination, for example, is described as if it is a precondition for any particular ethic but not itself one.[14] Yet, as we shall see, it does not usually refer simply to clients' ability to make their own decisions – perhaps irrational and non-constructive ones. "True" autonomy includes a person's ability to make decisions realistically, rationally, with sensitivity to others. These factors bring in value judgments, which remain unnoticed if "autonomy" alone is specified.[15]

In addition, procedures and client behavior are described in misleadingly benign ways which can blind us to what is really going on. Isolation of a client, for example, is sometimes described as time in the "quiet room." Client anger may be called "acting-out," which suggests that the fault lies with the client, when the response could be due to any number of non-psychiatric causes, including our biased assumptions.

Much of the language used in social work practice, then, serves to disguise our moral judgments by making us experts, by making clients into medical entities, or by making our procedures and goals appear value-free or benign. Some unethical practices, like office breaches of confidentiality which we view as resulting from carelessness, might more beneficially be seen as resulting from the way we use language and its implied view of the client and of ourselves. By distancing us from clients and describing issues as technical, our language encourages us to disrespect our clients in subtle ways – we may cease to treat them the way we ourselves want to be treated. They can easily become "cases to be handled" through "professional training." Our language becomes our thinking, and with this sort of thinking, the ethical and political dimensions disappear.

This supposedly non-ethical orientation, then, is tied to a much cherished social work ideal: the helpful-but-detached, value-free social worker, the opposite of the zealous, nineteenth-century reformer. I shall argue in this chapter, however, that the ideal of value-free counseling is impossible and dangerous. The non-political stand is misleadingly political, and the detached worker conveys values despite her detachment. If we do not recognize these assumptions, we (and our clients) cannot fully examine or challenge them. The relevant questions we must ask ourselves are: what ethical and political assumptions am I making? What point of view should I accept? How much of it should I convey openly to clients?

To answer these questions, we must turn to cases. Only by focusing on particular cases can we begin to understand the ways in which our therapeutic practice conveys our political and ethical views to clients.

In what follows, as little technical language will be used as possible. "Case" and "client" are retained, however, for want of better terms.

Case-studies

Case of Maria Garcia

> You are a white, middle-class, college-educated social worker, female, and your client, Maria, is a Chicana woman, aged twenty-four, who has recently moved to the city from a poor rural community in Mexico with her husband and two children, aged four and two. Maria was referred by her priest because she has been very depressed. She has frequent crying spells and has trouble taking any interest in her children. Her husband works long hours and they live in a three-room apartment in a large building. She does not see any point in going to a social worker and feels ashamed of it. Her husband does not like the idea but gave his approval because the priest suggested it and because his wife is unhappy but he refuses to see the social worker himself.

In this case, the attitudes of social worker and client are apt to differ on many topics: child-rearing, marriage, friendship, recreation, work, community, female professionals. Given their contrasting cultural backgrounds, even their concept of happiness and a meaningful life may differ sharply.[16] What, then, ought the social worker to do? Without extensive understanding of the client's point of view and of her culture, no understanding or help will be possible. But even with an understanding of the culture, to what extent ought the social worker to influence her client's views? For example, the social worker may believe that Maria will be helped by getting out of the house more, yet her belief runs counter to the Garcia's belief in the wife's proper role. Even the act of seeking help from a social worker, rather than solely from friends, family, or the church, involves a change of values for Maria and her husband.

On what basis should you try to influence Maria? Can a therapist help without radically transforming or misinterpreting a client's values? Is such transformation desirable?

Consider a second case of this general sort.

Case of Laura Johnson

> Suppose that you are a social worker who has a fundamentally different religious outlook from your client, Laura Johnson. Suppose that Laura is a fundamentalist Christian, very devout, whose whole life revolves around her religion. Suppose that you are an atheist. Your client is depressed. She spends a great deal of time in prayer and talks about her worthlessness in God's eyes. She is very strict with her fifteen-year-old daughter, in line with her church's teachings. Laura was referred for treatment by her doctor because of her depression.

Again in this case, the client's and social worker's values differ radically. The social worker's view of "mental health" is apt to include values that directly conflict with those of Laura Johnson. She may view Laura's religious beliefs as morbid and unhealthy, or may believe that mental health requires Laura to be less observant of her religion. At the very least, the social worker is unlikely to frame the goals of treatment in a religious context, since to do so is not accepted social work practice. Laura, however, strongly believes that goals should be framed in just such a context. In fact, standard social work practice assumes a secular context which violates the deepest beliefs of some clients. How does a social worker resolve this conflict of values? How does she respect both her client's ethical position and her own professional one?

Case of Jack

Both of the preceding cases present conflicts between the client's values and the social worker's professional values. The third case raises the question of whether or not "changing society" should be a social work goal.

In this case, the question posed is what the social worker should do about Jack's racism.[17] As a social worker, she is mandated to work against racism, but if a client does not request or wish this sort of help, then is she violating the client's self-determination?[18] On what criteria ought social workers to determine the issues of treatment?

> You are a white social worker employed in a neighborhood mental health clinic. Your client is a thirty-five-year-old white male, Jack, who is separated from his wife and two children, aged ten and eight. He has come to the clinic because he has trouble holding any job for more than a few weeks. He was referred to the clinic by a friend whose cousin once worked there.
>
> Jack has worked as a salesman for several automobile dealers but lost his last job over two months ago because he was often late for work. He is depressed and bitter about his marriage and about his limited visiting rights with his children. He dresses neatly and gives the impression of a gentle, soft-spoken man, though he describes sudden outbursts of temper which have cost him several jobs. He states that he wants help in being able to get and keep a job.
>
> As you talk to him on his first visit, it becomes clear that he has strong racist attitudes, particularly directed towards Blacks and Japanese. He uses racial slurs and relates several stories intended to demonstrate the moral inferiority of these groups.
>
> What ought you to do about his racism?

(1) Should Jack be allowed his racism – without intervention – if the attitude is clearly his own and he has thought about it, or is allowing self-determination in such a case tantamount to practicing racism?

(2) Where does a counselor draw the line between the "nonconstructive" attitudes and actions that she attempts to change and those she leaves undisturbed? What if the issue is not racism but instead sexism or heterosexism or educational elitism or religious bigotry?

If the case is modified, so that the social worker and the client are of different race, say the social worker is Black and the client white, these issues are further complicated. The racism may be more subtle and harder to talk about or confront. Also, in such cases the differences in outlook may well extend to almost every area, rather than being restricted to a few attitudes and thus be more like the case of Maria.

Cases of Jenny and Jane

The final two cases are drawn from C. Joffe's fascinating study of abortion counselors.[19] These cases reveal conflicts between the counselor's and the client's values, even when the agency, counselor, and client have agreed on the goals of counseling and the agency's political outlook. The cases reveal ways in which a social worker's personal values are apt to influence significantly the way she interprets her professional values.

Joffe's study was based on a year's study of Urban Clinic, a private nonprofit family planning agency in a Northeastern City. Urban has an abortion clinic which offers, on an outpatient basis, 150 first trimester abortions a week. The eight counselors give information and counseling to potential clients prior to the abortion, and accompany the recipients through the procedure itself.

The goals of counseling in this agency are to help each woman arrive at a reasoned decision with which she feels comfortable – either to have an abortion or not. If the woman decides to have an abortion, then the social worker is to give support through the abortion process.

> The official ideology of abortion counseling is that active engagement on the part of the client is all that is expected. Any decision is valid, as long as it is truly the client's – and not the counselor's or that of another outside party, such as a parent or boyfriend.[20]

Suppose that you are one of the counselors. Suppose either of the following two situations (taken in part from Joffe's article):

(A) You are counseling a thirty-year-old married woman, Jane, with a history of three prior abortions. She does not wish to talk about her feelings; she seems very much in control and wants information only about the procedures of this clinic. She wants children someday, "though now's not exactly the time."

(B) You are counseling a fourteen-year-old girl, Jenny, who, in spite of family pressures, insists on keeping her baby "so she can have something all her own to love."

If your values about abortion are such that you strongly disagree with one or both of these choices, then what ought your counseling role to be? If you believe that a woman should be able to choose abortion but that abortion should not be undertaken simply for convenience, then won't your counseling reflect your belief? Should it? You will want Jane to recognize that the decision is an important one and that inconvenience is an inadequate reason for having an abortion. In urging this point of view, however, you would be urging a particular ethical position, which goes beyond belief in self-determination of the client. Self-determination, then, would be defined to fit your own ethical outlook, although you might not recognize it.

In situations like the abortion examples, social workers will sometimes look for indications of pathology which can justify further questioning of the client. Social workers may also try to force a client to reexamine her decision, by questioning her in ways they would not probe someone they agreed with. In a case like Jenny, one social worker described her strategy:

> "I kept pushing her. She would sit there daydreaming about how cute the baby would be, and I kept asking her 'are you willing to get up in the night? Are you willing to give up running around with your girlfriends and partying? Do you realize it will probably be very hard to stay in school?'"[21]

As Joffe points out, "there is a fine line, at best, between such 'sharp questioning' on the part of the counselors and actually influencing the decision."[22]

These cases contrast sharply with the sort of "influencing" that takes place at a crisis pregnancy center in Baltimore, Maryland, a center that also offers counseling supposedly based on the self-determination of the client:

> Most women are attracted to the center by advertisements offering free pregnancy tests. . . . Women are shown a slide presentation that explains fetal development, the abortion process, and the emotional and physical consequences that often result from abortion. "A lot of girls want nothing to do with abortion once they see what's involved," says Barbara Hammond, director of the Baltimore center. . . . Staffed by concerned Christians, the center provides a "pro-life solution to the abortion problem." More than 80 per cent of the girls who enter the center choose to keep their babies.[23]

The contrast between the counseling in these two agencies illustrates the issue sharply: self-determination can differ radically, depending on the values, often unstated, of the social worker and agency.

We must ask, then, whether we should tell our clients how we are trying to influence them. We should also ask on what grounds we ought to have influence. If, for example, a woman wishes to commit suicide as her solution to being pregnant, a social worker will intervene actively. What is she is twenty-two years old and wants her tubes tied after an abortion? What if she wants to wait to make a decision about abortion until she is four-and-a-half months pregnant? On what basis do we decide that we ought to intervene in some decisions but not others?

The illusion of political neutrality

Each of the cases – dealing respectively with cultural and religious differences, racism and abortion – reveals the ethical and political nature of decisions therapists make. These judgments cannot be dismissed, however, as simply the result of selecting controversial cases, for the argument can be extended to any case whatsoever as I shall show.

Let us return to the first case, Maria, and examine it more closely. Maria has recently come to the United States from a small village in Mexico; her belief system and ways of living are apt to be radically different from those of her therapist.[24] Even the act of seeking help from a therapist, rather than from the church or a healer, involves a shift in values for her and her husband. Any therapeutic help thus inevitably brings in ethical and political assumptions about Maria's own cultural beliefs and the desirability of assimilation. Because the contrast is so sharp, the case illustrates how politically parochial even our most generally accepted goals and techniques may be.

Autonomy, for example, cannot be taken for granted as a goal of treatment. Maria equates autonomy with selfishness; she believes in the interdependency of family members, subordinate to the male authority, her husband.[25] This sort of belief is found even more strongly in many Asian immigrant families, where deference for authority and a primary group identity run strongly counter to the self-identification that is presupposed by autonomy, as the following example indicates.

> Mr B is a second-generation Korean high school student who experiences difficulty in getting along with his immigrant parents who violently object to his long hair. A worker's efforts in helping him to see that his need for wearing long hair has to do with his self-identity caused him to become more depressed and silent as he began to realize that he was satisfying his self-concept at his parents' expense. He withdrew from service after the first agency visit, clearly without having successfully resolved his conflict with his parents.[26]

In these cases, whatever the worker does involves taking a stand. Even encouraging a client to become aware of the conflict and to resolve it in his or her own way may run counter to the client's belief about how decisions should be made.

The way in which political judgments enter into the process is often subtle. To return to Maria, a skilled therapist will undoubtedly try to get her to talk about her experiences in Mexico and about the experience of being uprooted. The therapist's aim, over time, will be to help Maria figure out *what she wants.* The therapist's comments, however, will also be guided by her ideas of what is helpful and of what a therapist should do – which is usually to encourage autonomy, self-understanding, and individual development.

As therapists we tend to take for granted such goals as individual autonomy, self-knowledge, direct expression of emotion, equality, competitive assertiveness, and questioning of authority. We also tend to assume the superiority of these beliefs over others. These goals suggest a political perspective in which value is placed on the individual, competing freely within existing legal, economic and social institutions. We have seen how this perspective runs counter to Maria's cultural beliefs, which emphasize respect for tradition and authority, family cooperation over individual achievement, community interdependence and Christian virtues.

When confronted with cultural conflict, as in the case of Maria, we sometimes recognize the need to understand the assumptions we are making. We too rarely, however, draw the obvious conclusion: if our therapeutic goals presuppose a specific belief system in these cases, they must do so in all cases.

If we are going to promote autonomy as a general goal in therapy, we must understand what we mean by it, including the sort of society we are presupposing and alternatives to it.

One common therapeutic perspective is expressed by Breggin, who advocates autonomy connected to "the Jeffersonian and libertarian ideal of the individual's right to life, liberty and the pursuit of happiness."[27] He associates dependence with a totalitarian society and sees it as inconsistent with autonomy: "I do nothing which allows my patient to act dependently in relation to me."[28]

Dependence, however, might be connected, not to totalitarianism but to interdependence – a belief in socialist cooperation and ideals. Such a belief leads to a different sort of therapy from that which (1) promotes a non-dependent autonomy or (2) promotes dependence leading to autonomy within the existing social structure. The socialist ideal is one of mutual interdependence of equals in a classless, socialist economy, and autonomy is defined in terms of such cooperative activity.[29] Socialist therapists thus view clients as comrades in a common struggle.

We must decide, then, whether autonomy should be a goal,

and if so, what sort of autonomy – what sort of political perspective – we are advocating. We must become aware of the political and ethical assumptions implied by our goals.

Not only our goals, but also our particular ways of counseling – our insights – convey political and ethical judgments, as we shall see. To begin exploration of this issue, consider the following position.

> if a client completes insight therapy without a political consciousness, he can hardly be said to have a full understanding of himself. Whether a man works for himself, the government, the schools, private enterprise, or simply lives off his family or works for her family (as most women do), this person cannot reach any self-understanding without grasping his or her relationship to the immediate social and economic system and its place in the larger political system.[30]

In Maria's case, helping her cannot take place without helping her to understand her political reality. The problems of assimilation and racial discrimination cannot be avoided in therapy, because they figure so obviously in her life. With minority clients, we recognize that some of their problems are due to their position in the larger society, whatever our solution to them may be. Some therapists thus use their skills "to help people realize the source of their alienation and organize them to take action,"[31] while others urge people to accept their unfortunate status. Either way a therapist takes a political stand.

We need again to recognize that all clients, not just minority clients, are affected by political realities. And we need to ask whether we can give clients "insight" into their lives without taking some political point of view on their circumstances. If this sort of exploration of political issues is discouraged, won't the therapist's political views still affect treatment, but not be acknowledged?

Political issues, if labeled as such, are not usually taken up with clients, however. If a client wishes to discuss political issues – say abortion or socialism or racism – then of course a therapist will do so. And if a client's inner conflicts are reflected in political issues then, too, political discussion is relevant. In most other circumstances, however, bringing up political issues is considered *not only irrelevant but also unprofessional.*[32]

According to this position, a therapist has no business probing a client about racism, sexism, communism or any other issue, if the client does not wish it. Therapists are trained to help people with serious internal conflicts or pathology, and they are supposed to limit their interventions to such conflicts. Therapy should thus focus on developing client autonomy (with its values) but should avoid the suggestion of any more *particular* ethical or political point of view. According to this argument, once a therapist introduces particular values, there is no end to the different values that could be suggested.

I shall use the case of Jack to develop further the argument that as social workers we cannot avoid taking political stands with our clients. I shall argue in addition that current social work practice often encourages acceptance of a political stance that undermines central social work goals. We must therefore understand the political basis of our "insights" and reexamine our acceptance of them. My position is a controversial one which, at the least, I hope will generate further discussion of the ways our values affect counseling.

Let me begin by restating the ethical dilemma we face in counseling Jack. Jack's presenting problem is his unemployment; he is also racist but makes it clear that he is *not interested in discussing his racism.* If the therapist makes racism an issue, is she unfairly imposing her own views on the client? If she ignores the issue, is she then acting in a racist way? Is she in effect saying that unemployment is more important than racism?

One cannot argue simply that a therapist should undertake only those issues presented by the client, because as we know, often the "real" problems only become apparent to therapist or client in the process of therapy. Therapists must make some judgment about what the "real" issues are.

In theory at least, therapists would treat Jack's racism only if it was closely tied to his pathology. If Jack's racism is diagnosed, for example, as representing a deep absence of self-esteem, so that it is part of, say, a paranoid disorder, then the racism requires treatment as part of that disorder. If, however, it is seen as a garden variety of racism, unconnected to Jack's outbursts of temper and unstable unemployment record, then it is less likely to be a treatment goal.

I will argue that even if Jack's racism is not part of any established pathological disorder, we should not ignore it. If we do, we thereby take a political stand. To begin, consider how the *DSM III* and its diagnostic categories reflect political and ethical assumptions.[33] Many conditions designated as mental disorders do not count as "disorders" in the classic medical sense of an organic malfunctioning which results in malfunctioning of the individual and in diminished responsibility.[34] Mental disorders are differentiated from normal behavior by (a) their origin in the individual and (b) the individual unhappiness or maladaptation to society they cause.[35] Given the breadth and vagueness of this concept of mental pathology, alcoholism, schizoid personalities and anti-social personality disorders do not fit the criteria for mental disorder any better than racism does, yet they are included while racism is excluded.[36] Their origin is unclear, they do not necessarily make the individual unhappy, and they are destructive to society; all these criteria fit racism as well.

According to this line of argument, the decision not to treat racism reflects the tacit judgment that racism does not do severe harm to the individual or to society. At least, the harm it does is not considered as serious as that of anti-social behavior disorders with symptoms like truancy. The decision not to treat racism thus involves a political assumption about racism which itself has racist underpinnings.

Ironically, this sort of decision not to treat racism will be made by therapists who are committed to eradicating the effects of racism from the lives of their minority clients. The N.A.S.W. Code of Ethics, for example, stipulates that social workers should not practice or condone racism, although the implications of this for social work practice have not been made clear.[37] Therapists acknowledge that racism makes the lives of many minority clients practically unliveable and that it also constricts and distorts the lives of white individuals.[38] If, then, racism is not treated, while alcoholism and schizoid disorders are, it can be argued that the therapist is accepting the racist society and subtly promoting it through choice of treatment goals. Whether or not racism is raised and discussed in therapy, the therapist takes a stand on it, just as a therapist cannot help taking a stand on Maria's autonomy and assimilation.

One might still argue that important as racism is, a therapist must remain neutral in order to foster client autonomy – the client's capacity "to think for himself and to remain the absolute ethical and moral judge of his own thoughts and conduct."[39] On this argument, therapists cannot risk opening the way to imposing every sort of belief on the client. Particularly, given that we live in a society of diverse belief systems without adequate means for deciding among them, it may be said that we can only succeed in respecting the beliefs and dignity of others by maintaining neutrality.

We have already seen, however, that client autonomy itself reflects particular political assumptions which depend on the way autonomy is described. If, for example, Jack decides that he wants to set fire to his ex-boss's house to revenge his injured feelings, his decision will not be considered acceptable. While it is autonomous in the sense that he made it, it is not autonomous in the sense of being rational, realistic, and sensitive to others' rights.[40] His decision is (a) irrational in that his injured feelings are not well-grounded; (b) unrealistic in that it ignores the consequences to him; and (c) in violation of his boss's rights (if enacted). Jack's racism, however, is also (a) irrational, in that he does not have good grounds for his racist beliefs and feelings; (b) unrealistic in that it ignores the real characteristics of minority persons; and (c) in violation of the rights of others.

The second and third factors – understanding reality and taking some sort of responsibility towards others – are almost always part of therapeutic goals and cannot be defined apart from political and ethical assumptions. Any criteria for responsibility to others will reflect assumptions about the sort of society and sorts of relationships that ought to be validated. Any definition of reality will reflect assumptions about what economic, social and legal realities are significant. Any treatment plan, therefore, reflects political assumptions as well.

My argument, then, is that whether or not a therapist discusses racism, she is taking a stand. If we say that racism is not an appropriate issue for Jack's therapy, we thereby assume that racism is not grossly harmful to the individual or society and should only be discussed if it results in illegal actions. Such a view endorses the status quo and differs radically from that of, say, a socialist therapist who believes that our economic, social and legal institutions are exploitative and racist and that they attack an individual's self-worth. Both positions, and both treatment plans, assume a political point of view. A seemingly "neutral" view of "harm" or "society" or "racism" is instead a *particular* point of view and one which tacitly endorses the status quo. In this case, through its neutral stance, social work practice would tacitly perpetuate racism, even though such a stand contradicts its own goal of fighting racism.

The alternative in such situations is to treat Jack's racism without informing him of the goal. Manipulation of this sort, however, raises the question of whether it constitutes a subtle and unethical form of coercion, and this issue will be discussed in Chapter 5.

If every decision about racism involves political assumptions, then so will decisions about sexism, homophobia, communism, abortion, etc. They, too, will involve assumptions about what is harmful, what sort of society is desirable, what counts as true autonomy, and so on. Our choice of treatment goals and issues will thus unavoidably reflect our political and ethical outlook. "Neutrality" is supposed to protect the client from imposition of the therapist's values, but a value is conveyed nonetheless – the value of accepting the status quo.

I will argue that even if the social worker restricted herself solely to insight therapy or to psychoanalysis, the most non-directive of therapies, her therapeutic practice would still entail a political perspective. Consider again the case of Jack, who might undertake a traditional form of psychotherapy.

Jack has a history of unstable employment, poor family relationships and personal unhappiness. Suppose that you accept him as a private client in psychotherapy. Suppose for the sake of argument that you want to be as neutral as possible, assuming only the values of Jack's autonomy and fulfillment. In what ways will political assumptions necessarily be part of the therapy?

Breggin suggests three ways in which ethical and political assumptions will be present. (1) What view of the client's past does the therapy encourage? (2) What kind of relationship does the therapy foster? (3) What future behavior does the therapy encourage?[41] Through the questions asked and the support given, a therapist will encourage, and discourage, particular ways of thinking about the client's past and future – about his or her family, work experience, relationships, attitudes towards money, etc.

How will the therapist, for example, encourage Jack to view his unstable work history? Jack's work is a central concern of his, and the therapist will be exploring it with him – Jack's feelings about it, his experience of his parents' work, etc. While the therapist's comments will be based on what Jack says, the therapist will be suggesting to Jack ways of understanding his experience and will thus convey some sort of political perspective on work in our society. The alleged therapeutic neutrality translates either into acceptance of existing work patterns or subtle imposition of the therapist's own views about work.

A socialist therapist will see Jack's unstable work history as tied in part to the alienating nature of work in our society. This perspective will be central to the therapist's understanding of the *reality* Jack must confront to gain *insight* into his problems. Jack is doing a job that forces him to sell products he does not take pride in, to compete for commissions with his co-workers and to be divorced from any real decisions about his work.

Another therapist, who believes strongly in the free enterprise economic system, will also explore Jack's work history but will perceive *the reality* differently. She will want Jack to recognize the excitement of competitive business and the opportunities for advancement and satisfaction that this and other similar jobs offer. A liberal political perspective, implicit in standard practice, is close to this position.[42] If the goal is insight into conflicts about work, then that insight will come about within some context on work that the therapist helps provide. And that context includes basic assumptions about work and society.

Every issue will include similar sorts of assumptions. Suppose the therapist or Jack brings up Jack's unhappiness with his visiting rights. While the therapist will again focus on

Jack's own experience, the therapist's basic assumptions about families, feminism and children will influence the kind of questions asked and interpretations given. Therapists will differ on the *sort* of insight they offer.

Psychiatric casework will thus be significantly different depending on the political perspective one brings to it. Unfortunately, these differences are not generally acknowledged or discussed. The image of political involvement that persists is that of the therapist who "inappropriately" inserts personal opinions into discussion of a client's problem. The therapist is seen as focusing on her own issues rather than the client's, or as insensitively and rigidly applying a body of political theory, while losing sight of the individual client. This image, I think, goes back to nineteenth-century "do-gooders" who imposed their moral crusades on unwilling clients. In attempting to rid social work of coercive and narrowly moralistic behavior, social workers shifted from the *explicit* advocacy of values to more *subtle*, *implicit* advocacy of them. Coercion and moralistic behavior cannot be eradicated by misleadingly positing a value-free therapy. Political assumptions are unavoidable. By remaining insufficiently recognized, they may influence us and our clients in ways unknown to us and remain inaccessible to scrutiny and challenge.

All cases are more controversial than therapists generally acknowledge. While the political assumptions are easier to discern in cases like Maria's and Jack's, where issues of racism and cultural difference are prominent, they are nevertheless evident in other types of cases as well – cases of unemployment, juvenile delinquency, or marital unhappiness, to name a few. All the cases discussed reveal the need for careful reexamination of standard casework practice and of its hidden ethical and political assumptions. We must ask ourselves whose values are being promoted.

Recommendations

Let us return to the questions posed at the beginning of the chapter:

(1) If therapists inevitably convey values, what should they

advocate? What values ought to be the basis of therapy?
(2) What forms of persuasion are acceptable in conveying these values?

While these questions are usually answered together, separation helps to clarify them. This section will make some recommendations for therapeutic practice, in answer to the first question. The next chapter will take up the second question, that of persuasion, manipulation and coercion in casework practice.

How, then, does a social worker decide what values to adopt in casework practice? This book as a whole attempts to give social workers a *process* whereby they can answer the question. Each social worker should determine her point of view through comparing different political and ethical perspectives and through analyzing case decisions based on them. Through this process, the strengths and weaknesses of different positions emerge. In particular, flaws become apparent in the "neutral" stance that theoretically grounds much current practice.

Ideally, every plausible therapeutic model should be analyzed for its political presuppositions and compared with other models. This sort of comparison, however, is not easily made. There is no neat fit between different therapeutic models and different political systems. Consider again the basic questions that shape therapy:

(1) Who needs help?
(2) What is a successful outcome of treatment?
(3) How can we *best* achieve this outcome?

These questions can be reformulated to reflect their inherently political nature and to reflect the different sorts of judgments involved:

(1) What sort of people and what social conditions ought to be changed? Who should make these decisions?
(2) What personality traits and what social and political arrangements are desirable?
(3a) What sorts of relationships and of activities with clients bring about the desired results? (What works?)

(3b) Which of these relationships and activities are *acceptable*? (Is it ethical to do what works?)

Since ethical and political assumptions enter therapy at different levels, a therapist might make several different and even conflicting political assumptions. A therapist might, for example, use coercive methods with a client to free the client to act in non-coercive ways; EST therapy (Erhard Seminars Training) is allegedly one illustration of such coercion.[43] Many therapeutic models are consistent with several perspectives; psychoanalysis can be made consistent with a libertarian or socialist, a Christian or non-Christian perspective, for example. A full examination of different therapies and their underpinnings is not possible here. It would be a book in itself and I hope such a book will be written soon.

Several recommendations can be made, however, on the basis of the discussion in this chapter, and these recommendations lead into the issues of the subsequent chapters.

(1) Social workers ought to be aware of the political ramifications of the language used to describe cases and of the way services are set up. McKnight summarizes some of these issues, discussed earlier in the chapter:

> The language of modernized professional services mystifies both problem and solution so that citizen evaluation becomes impossible. . . . If I cannot understand the question or the answer – the need or the remedy – I exist at the sufferance of expert systems. My world is not a place where I do or act with others. Rather, it is a mysterious place, a strange land beyond my comprehension or control. . . . My very being is as client rather than citizen. My life and our society are technical problems rather than political systems.[44]

(2) Discussions of therapy by professional groups like social workers should include discussion of different political perspectives. Social workers should integrate political issues into talk about therapy, rather than letting such issues remain separate and neglected.

(3) A social worker ought to be clear about what political assumptions she is making. Only in this way can she be fully informed about the sort of therapy she is doing, its desirability

and its ramifications. These assumptions will be present in the general goals underlying her approach, in the techniques she employs and in the particular questions and insights she gives. All of these warrant careful examination by every social worker.

(4) More specifically, social work practice, dominated by psychiatric casework, suggests a political stance. Focus is on individual development and autonomy within our existing economic, social, and political institutions. These institutions, with regulation and reform, are believed to result in a society of social justice and equality. In fact, this reform figures little in actual casework with individuals. Actual practice, which implicitly supports the status quo, seems, at least sometimes, to undermine such goals as equality, cultural diversity, and empowerment of the poor. This perspective, then, because of its popularity and its lack of clarity about its political practice, particularly warrants examination and reformulation.

(5) Given the political nature of all counseling, each social worker ought to be much more explicit with clients about her political and ethical assumptions. While social workers stress the importance of making a contract and of involving clients in decisions, the contracts often do not include understanding of ethical and political commitments that will influence the therapist's approach, and the client remains ignorant of them. The myth of therapist neutrality has prevented this sort of revelation.

The last two recommendations are the most controversial of the five and raise serious questions that will be considered in the next chapter. If a social worker states her values to a client, will she thereby exert undue influence over the client? Is a therapist ever justified in working towards goals which are not revealed to the client? Is coercion in therapy justified? To examine these issues more closely, let us turn to the next chapter.

5 Directing the client: when is coercion justified?

> we recognize that it is possible, and at times justifiable, to coerce men in the name of some goal (let us say, justice or public health) which they would, if they were more enlightened, themselves pursue, but do not, because they are blind or ignorant or corrupt.[1]

> Some paradox in our nature leads us, once we have made our fellow men the objects of our enlightened interest, to go on to make them the objects of our pity, then of our wisdom, ultimately of our coercion.[2]

Coercion: a case-study

Annabelle Jones, twenty-five years old, with her nine-year-old daughter, Diane, lives in a crowded three-room apartment on the fifth floor of a public housing project. They are welfare recipients, recently moved to Boston, and were referred to the child welfare department by Diane's school. Annabelle is severely depressed and has been hospitalized twice (out of state) for psychotic breakdowns. She has few friends and no family in the area. She spends most of her time in the apartment watching television. The school department has filed complaints several times because of Diane's unkempt appearance, absences from school, hostile behavior towards teachers, and other inappropriate behavior. Neighbors have observed Diane wandering around the housing project late at night; she seldom plays with other children, preferring to remain at home or hide in the basement, which she does for hours at a time. Diane's teacher and the welfare worker both believe that Diane is neglected and that she is developing serious psychological problems.

The social worker has to decide what to do to help this family. She has seen Annabelle several times. Annabelle acts remotely cordial but says little – she appears to be without interest in most topics. Although she is affectionate toward Diane, she appears to have little real interest in her. Annabelle hopes that the social worker can provide more financial assistance but does not see the need for any other change.

What should the social worker do? Should she file for temporary custody of Diane on the basis of emotional neglect, even though neither Annabelle nor Diane want her to do so? Is such coercion justifiable?

Coercion is the use of force to bring about a desired result against a person's wishes or without the person's consent.[3] It violates a person's liberty, and since we value liberty, violation of it calls for justification. Liberty, however, can be defined in different ways and, as we have seen, it is not our only value: the good of society or the well-being of the person or others may take precedence over one person's liberty. Our justification of coercion, then, will depend on the other moral and political commitments we have. Most commonly a social worker will violate a client's liberty in order to achieve some other good. Involuntary foster home placements, for example, violate a parent's (and perhaps child's) freedom in order to bring about the seemingly greater good of protecting the child.

Several different terms are used to describe such actions: "coercion," "intervention," "paternalism," "manipulation." Paternalism originates from the idea of treating others in a fatherly way; parents interfere with their children's liberty in order to protect and help them.[4] It suggests that the action is justified by its benefit to the client. "Intervention" is a more general term used to refer not only to acts which protect or serve the best interests of the persons coerced but to acts which although they may violate the interests of one person protect others in society. "Manipulation" usually refers to bringing about a desired result without explicit force, thus seemingly non-coercively, but by indirect means, usually without the person's consent and against the person's wishes. Manipulation is in some ways the most controversial of the concepts, because it covers a wide range of behavior, from our ordinary manipulations of each other to lying to clients in order to get them to act as we want. Not surprisingly, social workers disagree about whether it is acceptable practice.

All four terms have been defined in a variety of ways.[5] "Coercion" does not necessarily entail, as "paternalism" does, that the action is believed to result in some greater good to the client. "Coercion," in fact, sometimes refers exclusively to unjustified interference in a person's life: if interference is justified, it is not coercion.[6] In this chapter, I shall use all four terms but shall refer chiefly to "coercion," because I find the term more graphic and clearer than the others. I shall use it to refer to any situation of force exerted over a client without the client's consent, justified or unjustified. Our question, then, is under what circumstances is coercion justified in social work practice?

The general issue is that of our responsibilities towards others: to what extent am I my brother's keeper? When should we help others (even if they do not want our help), and when are we simply meddling? If a child is drowning in a swimming pool, we clearly should do whatever we can to help. But we may have had experiences of intervening in others' lives – say, knocking on a neighbor's door when there are screams for help – only to find our help deeply resented.

Our responsibilities to strangers are vexing in a way those to family, friends, or employers are not. They puzzle us because our society is not a community of shared values or defined relationships and functions among its members. We do not have rules and customs to guide us. As stated by Fingarette, a philosopher writing about responsibility:

> I can speak for myself as a potential Samaritan. As far as custom goes, I am not sure what custom is, or was. Is it customary to rush to the aid of the injured or attacked? Or does one customarily run for a policeman or at least a telephone, letting the sufferer manage as best he can? If one has grounds to fear great financial liability, public embarrassment, or even mortal danger, does one intervene at all? – what is the custom here? I frankly don't know what the actual custom is.[7]

The social worker's situation is even more complex. She is mandated by society to intervene in strangers' lives, but the philosophical basis and limits of that intervention are not clearly spelled out nor agreed upon. The mandate is a kind of power, which is increased by other kinds of power – professional expertise, social class, legal authority. The social worker's offer of help thus carries a coercive element which must be considered in our moral evaluation of it. When should a social worker help, and what limits should we place on that help?

Analysis of coercion

In extreme cases we are able to agree about the limits of coercion. Forcibly removing a child from a home, for example, is justified if the danger to the child's life is great enough. Similarly, if a man suddenly becomes suicidal and incoherent, then hospitalizing him against his will is justified by his incompetence and the seriousness of the situation. At the other extreme, involuntary psychosurgery on patients in mental hospitals is in some cases clearly unjustified. It violates in a permanent way the patient's ability to think and to act and denies the patient any choice in the matter, sometimes for the dubious good of making life easier for hospital staff.

Most cases, however, like that of Annabelle and Diane, have an inherent messiness that defies any neat moral analysis. Is a social worker, for example, justified in taking a child away from parents when the harm is primarily emotional and not physical? Should a patient in a mental hospital ever be forced to undergo drug therapy? Should alcoholics be kept in rehabilitation programs against their will? On what basis should these cases be decided?

In order to make an informed decision, we must sort out the relevant ethical issues. The following questions can serve as a rough guide in an analysis.[8]

(1) What values are violated by the coercive act?
(2) What is the good of the coercive act?
(3) Is the person competent to make the decision?
(4) How does the power of the coercer affect our evaluation of the coercive act?
(5) What is our overall evaluation?

Let us examine the questions more closely and see how they apply to the case of Annabelle and Diane.

(1) What values are violated by the coercive act?
Any coercive act, by definition, will violate someone's freedom. To evaluate the coercion, we need to know both what freedom is violated and what sort we value: freedom from interference by others in our private lives, freedom to have goods like property or employment, freedom to act or think in religious ways, or whatever. Any concept of freedom will be based on assumptions about how we should be permitted or forbidden to act towards others. If, for example, we take Diane away from her mother, we violate Annabelle's freedom to make decisions about her daughter's life in order to protect Diane's well-being or her right to life (a prerequisite for freedom). If we hospitalize Annabelle against her will to treat her depression, we violate her freedom to make decisions about her own life and violate her privacy as well. Our actions therefore reveal our beliefs that certain freedoms are more important than others. In our society today, the most important sorts of freedom are generally referred to as "rights" – the right to privacy, free speech, assembly, and so on. When a particular freedom conflicts with other freedoms or with other values in the society, then we must decide which has priority, and our decisions often reflect basic differences in political perspective.

A coercive action may violate other values besides freedom. Removing Diane from her home may, for example, violate a trust established between the social worker and the mother. The value of trust will need to be included in the deliberation.

(2) What is the good of the coercive act?
Our calculation of the good of the coercive act usually assumes a utilitarian basis: the concern is with evaluating the *consequences* of the coercive act for society as a whole. How great is the benefit that will result?

Violating an individual's liberty may be justified, for example, because it results in greater overall liberty. A school placement for Diane (against her will) might result in making her more self-reliant and independent, and these consequences would affect our evaluation of the coercion. Even if the school placement does not result in increased autonomy for Diane, it will seemingly be justified if it has other compelling results – if it makes Diane happier or prevents her from damaging property in her community.

It may also be justified on the grounds that it compels Annabelle and Diane to take responsibility for their actions. This justification may be made not in terms of any actual benefit to the client but in terms of the value to society of individual responsibility: the intent of the coercive act is to force the client to take responsibility for his or her actions.

Coercive acts are thus justified by the good consequences that result from the coercion – the overall well-being to the client, others and society itself. An informed decision, then, requires an understanding of the sort of society we are trying to create.

(3) Is the person competent to make the decision?

If the client is not competent to make a decision, then going against the client's wishes appears more easily justified because of the incompetence. Still, we must decide what constitutes incompetence. Is a severely depressed mother on welfare, for example Annabelle, incompetent to decide her child's well-being? If so, we must also decide who should make the decision – family member, the courts, social worker? And if coercion is justified, what limits should be placed on it?

In such cases, we should consider what the person would do, if competent. Would the person consent to the interference if he or she had more information, was fully rational or was in other ways competent to decide?[9] For example, although Annabelle may be too depressed to make any decision about Diane, we may be able to infer from her prior history that she would want a particular sort of help, if she could rationally make a decision.

In cases of incompetence, we must be particularly careful that we are not simply imposing our wishes on a client, without due justification.

(4) Do situations of power over a client's life set up a context in which interference in a client's life must be differently evaluated?[10]

Because of our power we must be careful that we do not impose on clients standards that others in society do not have to meet. For example, social workers may be able to insist that clients meet standards of day-care arrangements or of marital stability that are higher than for other members of society, and they can do this because of their power over clients' financial security or over the custody of their children.[11] In the case of Annabelle and Diane, therefore, the social worker must evaluate whether she is imposing standards of cheerfulness and good housekeeping which are unwarranted.

To take this further, because social workers have power over clients' lives, manipulation that may seem innocent in some contexts may amount to coercion – to forcing action on a client. This issue will be examined later in the chapter.

To give another example, in prison settings, persons have so little control over their lives that interventions which are not controversial in most situations (therapy or experiments) may result in further reducing prisoners' autonomy and may therefore be unjustified, even with prisoners' consent.

(5) What is the overall evaluation?

With this final question, the ethical and political nature of the process becomes most apparent. We must somehow add together the different factors, yet this often seems impossible. How are we, for example, to add together our answers to our first two questions?

(1) What values are violated by the coercive act?
(2) What is the overall good of the coercive act?

Our answer to the second question, by focusing on consequences of an action, may conflict with our answers to the first, which focuses on values (like freedom) for their own sake. We may not be able to add together our answers because they are incompatible – one rules out the other. We live with these incompatible moral perspectives in our society.[12]

In some cases, however, our inability to resolve a case dilemma arises from not adequately defining our own ethical and political perspective. Consider again question 2: "What is the overall good of the coercive act?" This question usually assumes a utilitarian basis, though we know it is just one of several possible ethical views. We might have asked instead: "What virtues are promoted by the coercive act?" or "What sorts of empowerment and equalization of class differences does it achieve?" Depending on the ethical perspective we assume, we will ask and answer the question differently. We must decide, for example, whether by "overall good" we mean the best consequences for society given our economic and social arrangements, the best consequences for creating a classless society, or the best way to create virtuous persons, apart from other consequences.

Understanding our perspective is essential to any answer we give. In weighing the factors for and against coercion, we will inevitably frame the questions and answers in a larger context – of what counts as harm or good or freedom, and thus of what counts as a desirable society. Our answers to the questions are only helpful if we understand the larger context. If freedom is outweighed by well-being, for example, then we need to know what social ideals and institutions are implicit in these concepts of freedom and well-being.

How, then, are we to apply these questions to the case of Annabelle and Diane? Should we forcibly intervene? Is coercion justified?

The overall benefit or harm of the intervention, even for Annabelle and Diane, cannot be determined with any assurance. The harm to Diane is primarily emotional rather than physical, and its long-term effects are not predictable with any accuracy: the positive effects of school placement (psychological help, better environment, physical safety) are uncertain, as are the negative effects of separation (stigma, self-blame, financial hardship, loss of family).

Even supposing that we assessed accurately what is most beneficial to the *clients* involved, we must still weigh that assessment against the benefit and harm (including cost) to the agency, society and to the social worker herself. Often, the monetary cost to the agency or state rules out the most desirable course of action. School placements are frequently prohibitively expensive or unavailable. The cost to the social worker may also rule out what would most benefit the client. The social worker, for example, may not have time to supervise Annabelle and Diane adequately. The social worker is responsible to the client, agency, society, profession and colleagues, and these responsibilities are hard to make commensurable.

Besides these problems, there are those of determining Annabelle's competence. Although Annabelle seems rational in her conversation, she seems unconcerned about Diane's behavior. Annabelle has been hospitalized for depression before, and her current depression may distort her reasoning. How much understanding or display of rationality is required to show competence? Such are the kinds of problems that dominate social workers' attention.

Further, the social worker must consider conflicts between ethical values themselves – in particular, well-being versus personal freedom. Removing Diane from her mother might be of indisputable benefit to everyone involved and yet still not be justified, because it would violate Annabelle's freedom to make her own – good or bad – choice. It is even possible that Annabelle might later agree that sending Diane away improved their lives but also argue that the action was unjustified because it violated her freedom. We too often assume that if lives are improved by social intervention, the intervention is thereby justified.

Any decision you make will reflect beliefs about the nature and importance of freedom relative to other values. You might decide, for example, to obtain legal custody in order to place Diane in a residential school if the damage to Diane is severe enough. On this argument, even though it will be painful for the family and will violate the mother's freedom of choice as a parent, the potential good to Diane might seem to outweigh that freedom. Diane is not old enough to make a fully rational decision about her future, and the mother, while competent, does not understand the seriousness of the situation. The intervention takes away from the mother an important choice and significantly alters her life but the interference with freedom is a temporary one and does not violate the mother's custody in any permanent way.

If you make this decision, you are probably assuming that society's responsibility to individual children is greater than its commitment to parental freedom. You are also putting higher value on personal well-being and care for others than on individual freedom. And you are giving a high priority to the social worker's special knowledge and expertise in evaluating the lives of others.

A strong counter-argument can be made for working with Annabelle and Diane in the home and not going against the wishes of the parent. Several different political underpinnings are compatible with such a decision. To give one example, you might assume that individual freedom is of such high value and so important for individual self-respect and the well-being of society that it should not be violated except in situations of extreme physical danger or incompetence. You might argue that particularly since Annabelle and Diane are poor and feel unempowered, it is important not to reinforce their powerlessness by coercive actions. If they were middle-class and wealthy, you might not be able to impose your decision on them.[13] You will attempt to provide supportive services and thus increase their sense of freedom, empowerment and well-being. Well-being is invoked by either decision, but freedom and equality are more central components of the latter than of the former. The decision to keep Diane home might also be made by a strict libertarian, who would argue similarly for freedom but not necessarily for empowerment of the poor. The patterns of our decisions will reflect these differences, though we may be only dimly aware of them.

I am not arguing here for the relativism of values – that any decision is equally justifiable. Some decisions, such as placing Diane in a school and preventing her mother from seeing her, can be ruled out by the overwhelming arguments that can be made against it, given basic values of freedom and equality. There is, however, no way to establish a single right decision in this situation. Informed discussion of the alternatives must include discussion of different political assumptions and we have no definitive way to establish the truth of one such perspective over all others. Some political assumptions are more adequate than others, however, and they can only be determined by including them in social work discussions. Doing so will help clarify some social work disagreements and will result in a better understanding of the basis of particular decisions.

In justifying coercion, two factors need particularly careful evaluation and both are evident in this case. They concern the *power* of the social worker and the *competence* of the client.

The expertise of the social worker is a kind of power; the expert assumes that she has superior knowledge and skills in evaluating a client and in proposing changes. Because of our "superior knowledge," we may be tempted to assume without justification that clients are lacking in competence – we may judge a client incompetent by virtue of his or her role (the dependent, needy, bewildered supplicant). We may thus too quickly assume that Annabelle does not fully understand her own problems or the implications of Diane's misbehavior. The issue is complex, because in many cases clients in fact have limited competence due to mental problems or to their age. Criteria of competence need to be clearly spelled out and constantly reevaluated, to avoid unwarranted assessments of incompetence.

If the social worker and Annabelle have different value systems, there is also the danger that differences in values will figure negatively in the social worker's assessment of competence. We must understand and question the assumptions we make about clients' diminished capacity, for these evaluations can radically alter their lives.

In many cases the social worker has power over clients not only because of her expertise but because of inequalities in society based on social class, race, professional status, and access to powerful institutions. In such situations, coercive actions require particularly strong justifications. Because they can be undertaken by a social worker who knows that the client cannot successfully oppose them, they can reinforce the client's powerlessness and may be undertaken when unwarranted.[14] If Annabelle, for example, is Black and poor, the chances that a court will give custody of Diane to the state are greater than if Annabelle were a white, middle-class woman with her own lawyer. The legal system does not always serve as an adequate check on a social worker's power in cases of coercion. Coercion may still be justified but the effects of the social worker's power and client's powerlessness must be carefully evaluated.

In some social work settings, coercion is a standard, accepted part of the work. Drug and alcohol rehabilitation programs often use coercive behavior modification techniques: a client must do required tasks in order to obtain "privileges" which are rights in the larger society – freedom of movement, access to entertainment, etc. We must carefully monitor these coercive techniques, particularly if clients have not consented to their use (as with the mentally retarded and with court-ordered treatment). We sometimes too readily assume that if the treatment seems to work, it is thereby justified.

There is yet another danger to coercion in these settings: its *regular* and *accepted* use can erode our awareness that we are even using it. We may therefore cease to question coercion and extend its use to situations in which it is not justified. Particular vigilance and constant questioning are required in these situations.

In summary, then, to justify coercion we should carefully evaluate at least the following five questions and their political and ethical underpinnings:

(1) What values are violated by the coercive act? How seriously is freedom violated? Are other values violated, such as trust or personal integrity?
(2) What is the good of the coercive act (to the client, others, agency, society)? What ethical perspective does our answer assume?
(3) Is the client competent to decide? If not, how should a decision be made? Who should make the decision? How is "competence" defined?
(4) How does the power and position of the social worker or the institutional setting affect our evaluation of the coercive act?
(5) What is the overall evaluation of the above factors? What is our political perspective?

Manipulation

The case of Annabelle and Diane Jones also raises questions about the ethics of manipulation: when does manipulation constitute covert coercion and when, if ever, is it justified? Covert coercion is the unacknowledged or disguised use of force to bring about a desired result. If Annabelle "voluntarily" agrees to place Diane in a residential school but does so only because of an implied and misleading threat of a court custody battle, then her agreement is based on covert coercion. To give another example, suppose that the social worker describes the placement as a regular boarding school in order to secure Annabelle's consent, when in fact it is a residential treatment center, for which Annabelle might not give permission.

Covert coercion deserves our special attention. While any act of coercion violates a person's freedom, covert coercion violates it two-fold: the client is moved to act in some way counter to his or her wishes but, being unaware of the coercion, cannot choose to resist it. If such coercion is the only way to prevent irreparable harm to a client, it is sometimes justified. Suppose, for example, that only by lying to an irrationally angry husband can you prevent him from finding and killing his wife. In other situations, however, covert coercion may enable a social worker to force a course of action on a client without the additional check of law or some other authority, as in the child custody case above; the coerion is achieved in a hidden way that remains unexamined, often even by the social worker.

We must ask, then: what counts as covert coercion? When is covert coercion justified? Is every form of manipulation an example of covert coercion?

The ethics of manipulation poses particularly difficult problems, in part because the concept itself is so slippery. It is loosely characterized as indirectly forcing a course of action on a person, usually without their knowledge and against their probable wishes.[15] However, we use "coercion," "intervention," "paternalism," and "manipulation" in a variety of overlapping ways, as we saw earlier in the chapter. We sometimes find manipulation indistinguishable from persuasion, at other times indistinguishable from coercion.

We know, for example, that almost everyone uses manipulation at times. Parents manipulate their children, particularly when they are very young, while children try and sometimes succeed in manipulating their parents. Both parents and children may be aware or unaware of their manipulations. Wives similarly may manipulate their husbands, and husbands, wives. In professional contexts a certain amount of manipulation is accepted practice. Doctors manipulate their patients; teachers, their students; social workers, their clients. Again, although we usually assume that the professional consciously manipulates the unknowing client, the awareness may be reversed. A client may know, for example, that a worker's biased questions about her life of prostitution are manipulative, without the worker saying so or even being aware of it herself.

Situations of manipulation, then, include wide variations in (1) the awareness of manipulator and manipulated; (2) the power differences between them; (3) the degree to which choices are foreclosed; (4) the good to be gained; and (5) our moral evaluation of the action. We tend to view manipulation more tolerantly when it is used against a more powerful person or when it will result in some overriding good.

Manipulation in social work is justified in the same way parents justify their manipulations of their children: it is for the person's good. Such manipulations in social work are common, although not usually labeled as such: social workers formulate client goals which are unacknowledged to clients, and attempt to "persuade" or change them without their explicit consent. This includes withholding, distorting, and arranging information for effect, as well as implied threats. Such manipulation is hard to evaluate, because it is often subtle. It may not involve clear-cut action against the client's wishes, which themselves may be vague or contradictory.

In evaluating manipulation, however, we must remember that social workers have considerable power over clients' lives, and thus their manipulative acts often carry a coercive element. We must question whether social workers' authoritative position makes their manipulative acts covertly coercive and thus usually unjustified. I shall argue that manipulation should usually be avoided and needs always to be carefully monitored. If coercion is necessary, it should generally be undertaken *with the client's knowledge.* Otherwise, social workers may be able covertly to force actions on clients that society and clients would not allow if these actions were made explicit.

In order to examine the ethics of manipulation more closely, consider again my conclusions drawn at the end of the last chapter and see how they apply here. I argued that therapeutic neutrality is a myth and that therapists' basic ethical and political commitments necessarily shape therapy. I suggested in conclusion that therapists have a responsibility to inform clients of these commitments so as not to influence them without their knowledge and consent. To put this another way, manipulation should be replaced by explicit discussion whenever possible.

My points are as follows: if a therapist informs a client of these commitments, then (1) the client can make an informed choice about whether or not to see the therapist. The therapist thus offers the client greater freedom of choice than if the therapist posits a mythical, neutral stance. (2) If the client decides to see the therapist, the client will know what commitments shape the therapy and be in a better position to discuss them openly and to disagree. (3) If a client has no choice except to see this therapist, at least the client will know the ways in which the therapist is attempting to influence him or her. This confers on the client a basic respect and dignity which helps to mitigate the coercive effects of forced treatment.

At least four sorts of counter-arguments can be made against the position of informing a client of relevant values: (1) that doing so is impossible; (2) that clients are not competent to understand these values; (3) that the position is itself coercive; and (4) that it undermines the help given to the client. Let us consider these counter-arguments and then turn to specific cases to examine the issue further.

Gaining the sort of informed consent recommended above is unrealistic according to one counter-argument because of the nature of therapeutic help. In many cases, therapists cannot predict what goals and techniques will be appropriate, and even if they could, relating them to a client will be overwhelming and misleading. Clients, generally, are not interested in understanding technical aspects of therapy. And informed consent is not possible anyway: when the goals of therapy are general – to help a client to become more autonomous or fulfilled – it will be impossible to know in advance what form that will take or what it will really be like for the client. Where goals are more specific, they are apt to change in the course of therapy. In addition, even if a therapist attempts to inform a client about values, a therapist's stated values are not necessarily a reliable guide to what her values are in practice.

The second counter-argument is that clients are not competent to understand these values. Often, clients are in severe crisis and barely able to function. Discussion of the therapist's commitments thus seems inappropriate and a waste of time.

The third and fourth counter-arguments are interrelated. Informing a client of the therapist's values will be coercive in at least some cases, because of the client's susceptibility to suggestion. As Whittington states, "the more successful we are [in building a relationship] the more susceptible to our influence the client is likely to become."[16] A client will want to please the therapist or will rely upon the therapist's superior knowledge and expertise and so will unquestioningly accept the therapist's suggestions. In other cases, a client may be so desperately unhappy or vulnerable that she or he will accept any suggestion made. Alternatively, if a client is afraid of the therapist because of her power and position, the therapist's explicitly stated commitments may be viewed as a demand or threat when they are not. In all of these cases, informing the client of the therapist's commitments will be in effect a form of coercion and will undermine the client's autonomy and self-exploration. In addition, in some cases the client's ignorance of goals or techniques may be essential to the effectiveness of therapy.

These counter-arguments help to illustrate the ambiguities of informed consent and therapeutic power in counseling, but they remain unconvincing as justifications of manipulation, as I shall argue.

(1) Although we cannot spell out all the goals and techniques in a therapeutic relationship, it does not follow that we should say nothing. Broad political and ethical assumptions shaping a therapist's interventions can be partially disclosed at the beginning, so that a client will be encouraged to seek information if the client wants to know more. Many feminist and some socialist therapists already do this.[17] With specific issues that come up during therapy, a therapist can and should indicate her commitments if the client wants to know them. *How much* a therapist reveals must depend upon the relationship and the client's ability to process such information. In the abortion case (Chapter 4), for example, the therapist could indicate openly that she has strong doubts about the client's

decision to have a fourth abortion. If she does not make her position clear yet in effect is trying to persuade a client of her position, then she is acting coercively, given the power of her position.

(2) Clients may be informed of a therapist's commitments and still not fully understand what they are consenting to. This will certainly be true of severely disturbed clients. With most clients, however, we cannot know the extent to which they can understand unless we give them the chance. The greater danger is that we will assume our clients cannot understand when they can, and thereby disrespect them.

(3) and (4) According to the third and fourth arguments, while disclosing values is not unrealistic, it is undesirable. If you inform a client of your values about abortion, for example, then you may influence the client to accept or defy your position solely on the basis of your authority, or make the client feel judged and condemned. The client's attention will be focused on the therapist's view rather than on an open-ended exploration of all positions.

I argue, however, that if the therapist is trying to influence clients and does not reveal her goals, then she acts coercively and thereby limits clients' choices. While clients may simply accept what a therapist says – or react against it – there is the equal danger that they will accept a therapist's views without realizing they are doing so. Let us examine this argument.

Informing clients of values is considered dangerous because of the therapist's power: therapists can often impose actions on their clients, and clients often act to please a therapist. In fact, however, evidence is inconclusive about how "suggestible" clients are. Several studies suggest that a client is most apt to trust a therapist when their values are similar and is therefore probably more "suggestible" in such cases. When the values and cultural differences are great – as is often the case with middle-class social workers and working-class clients – then clients are less apt to trust a therapist's opinion and are less apt to be unduly influenced by it.[18]

In these cases, one might still argue that clients will interpret the therapist's opinions as demands or threats because of the therapist's power over clients' lives; one might argue that in fact the more unequal the relationship, the greater the possibility that revealing values will be coercive. But I argue that in such cases, at least clients will know where they stand. Resorting to manipulation increases the power of the therapist, because clients often will not know how therapists are trying to influence them.[19] Knowing the therapist's values can result in an exchange of views, or at least to self-protection by the client, rather than the imposition of undeclared values.

Probably the most commonly accepted argument against revealing values in psychiatric casework is that it will undermine or distort transference. On this argument, helping the client is closely tied to the development and resolution of transference: in the relationship between therapist and client, a client transfers important early relationships onto the therapist and the therapist's task is to analyze these relationships with the client, not to divert discussion to the therapist's own values.[20]

Drawing on a related psychoanalytic explanation, one could argue that manipulation is the only effective way to help clients, given the nature of the unconscious. Clients will resist recognizing or accepting appropriate goals because of their repressed conflicts and can only be changed in desirable ways through various forms of benign manipulation which develop transference and thereby modify the unconscious.

In some cases, if this or some similar sort of psychoanalytic description is true, manipulation may indeed be the only appropriate response. For some clients who are confused and depressed, for example, manipulation may be the only way to begin to get them to feel positive self-esteem, seemingly against their wishes. Even here, however, we must be aware of what situations we see as enhancing self-esteem and be open to making clients aware of our assumptions.

This sort of justification of manipulation also depends on the accuracy of the psychoanalytic explanation and of its particular application. A full examination of psychoanalytic theories cannot be given here, but we should be cognizant of the many disagreements about their validity and appropriate application. In addition, we must be aware of other dangers of these positions: assuming that we know clients' "real" interests better than they do because they are blocked by unconscious repressions and dismissing their objections as resistance. While in some cases this may be justified, we may end up not taking clients' views seriously and impose our own unjustified view of their happiness, as well as of their problems.

There are other related arguments against the manipulation of clients in these situations. (1) Since therapists' values will affect their analyses of clients' problems, as we saw in the last chapter, clients can only fully know the sort of insight they are receiving, if therapists say something about their values, and many clients will want such information. (2) If a client asks about a therapist's values, a therapist's non-disclosure can be as much of a diversion as her disclosure. The professional mandate not to disclose seems suspiciously self-serving.

In addition, disclosing values forces the social worker to be aware of her own values and she will thus be more aware of the ways she may unjustifiably influence a client. She is also more apt to maintain respect for the client, because such disclosure limits the opportunities for manipulation.

Once we recognize the ethical and political dimensions of counseling, the justifications for manipulation appear inadequate in most cases. It is often a form of covert coercion. It undermines respect and empowerment of clients, goals central to social work practice. In the rest of this section, manipulation will be considered as it applies to some of the cases presented in Chapter 4.

Consider again the *Case of Maria*, presented on page 87. Suppose that you are a feminist and know that your feminist beliefs will affect in some way your advice to Maria.[21] You believe deeply that she needs to develop her own sense of self and some independence and confidence apart from her husband. If you tell her this, however, you believe that she will stop seeing you. She may misinterpret anything you say about your basic assumptions, even if you avoid the word "feminist." She is suspicious of you and ready to find an excuse not to see you, yet you know that she desperately needs help.

In order to help her, you have been taught that you must focus on developing a relationship – on helping her to feel comfortable and to trust you. Doesn't this sort of situation justify not revealing your goals or only stating them in a misleading way?

To reveal your goals even in a general way will seemingly undermine the effectiveness of therapy. On the other hand, Maria can only disagree with the help you offer if she knows what it is. By not telling her, you prevent her from being able to make an informed decision. She also may feel more comfortable knowing the social worker's values than having to guess them. After all, the fact that the social worker is, say, a white female professional itself reveals to her that the social worker's values are different from her own. In addition, because Maria is limited in her resources to fight for her own views – she is a poor, Spanish-speaking woman in a racist, sexist, English-speaking society – she should be given every opportunity to know the ways in which those with power over her are attempting to change her life, so that her power is not further eroded.

If Maria cannot afford to go elsewhere for help, and is therefore in some sense "forced" to see you, you must be particularly careful not to manipulate her.

In Maria's case, manipulation is not justified from any of the perspectives considered earlier. It violates her freedom to choose and increases her powerlessness, on the uncertain ground that otherwise she will refuse help. Even if she did refuse help, it is not clear that such a decision would result in serious harm.

The *Abortion cases*, discussed on pp. 90–2, bring out other aspects of manipulation. Counselors were to convey that any decision for or against abortion was acceptable, as long as it was the client's own decision and not illegal.[22] In practice, however, if the client's values conflicted strongly with the social worker's, the worker attempted in subtle ways to change the client's views without making her intention explicit. One social worker, for example, questioned critically a woman who wanted a fourth abortion. Was such questioning legitimate persuasion or coercion?

The social worker might argue that if she had revealed her position, the client might not have continued the conversation, and so the worker might have lost the opportunity to persuade her. She might argue further that the questioning itself was adequate to reveal her bias.

I argue, however, that by not revealing the goal to the client the social worker did not have to confront openly the conflict between her values and the client's; she could remain self-deceived about her goals. In addition, the client was not given the opportunity to refuse such counseling nor to confront directly the issue of difference in outlook. These cases suggest how manipulation can serve to protect the worker, rather than to help the client.

The cases also reveal the blurred line between manipulation and persuasion; in Carole Joffe's study of abortion several of the encounters seem clearly to involve a coercive element because the social worker's actual goal differed from the goal she expressed to the client.[23] This blurred line can lead social workers to gloss over and not explicitly address the issue of manipulation. Instead they stress the importance of "client participation," which remains conveniently vague, or talk about "manipulation" without attempting to distinguish its justified from unjustified use.

Even if a social worker explains her position to a client, her *stated* position may not reflect her position *in practice*. Explicit disclosure of values, however, may serve to make workers more aware of discrepancies between what they say and how they act.

One last case will be presented which dramatically poses the issue of justifying manipulation. In this case, the counselor lies to the client to prevent him from harming himself. Is such lying justified? While it is not as common as other sorts of deception in therapy, lying, by its blatant nature, serves to bring out important dimensions in our understanding of manipulation. It particularly highlights issues about the nature of the relationship between therapist and client.

Lying to a client

The following case, abbreviated here, appeared in the *Boston Globe*:

A Boston Police Cadet, Costine, was answering emergency

phone calls. He received a call from an unidentified man who said he was going to commit suicide. "I'm holding a shotgun to my head." The man's wife had taken their two girls, one and two years old, and gone off to Florida. The man said that he was losing his apartment, he had no money, and no one cared about him. Costine said that he wanted to help. The man hung up soon after, being afraid that the call would be traced, but called back a few minutes later. He said that he had filed a missing person report. Costine suggested that he come down to the station and make out a criminal complaint. He describes the rest of their conversation as follows:

"He told me he lived at a Princeton Street address and then said he had barricaded the door."

"I immediately gave the address to Sgt Gill who ordered six cars, including two sergeants, detectives, patrolmen, and an ambulance to the address."

"While that was going on, I told the man I, too, was married and that I was in a similar situation. (Costine is single). But I told him that though my wife had left me, we had no children. "So, you see, I'm going through the same thing you're going through. I talked to my priest, why don't you talk to me?"

"I told him that I had to get a complaint out against my wife, but that I didn't even know where she had gone. He said, 'Well, now you know what it's like,' adding that he felt he could trust me. He said he knew I wouldn't call the police on him, but I have a job to do, and I did it."

Costine said that at that point he could hear someone ringing the man's doorbell. "He told me he had looked out the window and the police were there, that I was a liar, that I had sent the police and then hung up."

Costine called back five minutes later and was able to persuade the man to open the door for the police.[24]

Was Costine justified in lying? Was he justified in sending the police to the home? Let us use the five questions outlined earlier to examine how the case might be argued.

(1) What values are violated by the action? Costine's action is dishonest in itself regardless of its consequences. It violates a basic respect for others, by treating the suicidal man dis-

honestly.[25] In addition, the act may cause harm by creating distrust, both in the man and in others. The man, when he learns of the deception, may feel betrayed and try again to commit suicide. Others, reading of the episode in the *Globe*, may in the future not believe what police and other counselors tell them. It also violates the man's freedom to decide what to do without interference of police, since Costine did not inform him of the real purpose behind keeping him engaged in conversation, although this justification seems far-fetched in this case.

(2) What is the benefit of the action? The action is beneficial in that the man's life will most likely be saved. Also, since the man is threatening immediate suicide, there may be insufficient time for a non-deceptive kind of intervention. One might argue that given the seriousness of the consequences, one should do whatever is necessary to assure the man's safety.

(3) Is the man competent to decide for himself? The man appeared to be distraught and irrational. His decision seemed an impulsive one and not rationally grounded. Given his irrationality, one might argue that any sort of communication to which he will respond is justified, since he will not necessarily respond to rational argument. This would support Costine's action.

(4) How does the power and position of the counselor affect our evaluation of the action? Since the police cadet did not have any prior relationship to this man and was simply taking emergency calls, one might argue that the violation of trust was not as serious as if it had involved an on-going therapeutic relationship. In addition, by calling the police the man is revealing a desire for help and an awareness of how the police might act under these circumstances.

(5) What is the overall evaluation of the above factors? The overall evaluation will depend upon the weight you give to the conflicting values and upon your fundamental ethical and political perspective. Consider three resolutions, briefly sketched.

(a) If you put highest value on individuals' freedom from interference by others, then you may believe the only justification for lying would be the man's incompetence. His welfare is his to determine, and our ideas about what is good for him should not take precedence. Since you may be able to persuade him without lying, and since he may be competent, lying is not justified. Szasz, in his emphasis on freedom, maintains a position similar to this.[26]

(b) You may also be opposed to Costine's lying, but for different reasons, if, for example, you put highest value on the trust, respect, and interdependence of individuals. Lying and the distrust it creates can only be justified in extreme situations where some great evil will result and no other remedy is possible. Again, because the man appeared open to talking on the phone and himself initiated the calls, lying seems unjustified.

(c) If you put highest value on the man's welfare, defined as his being a happily functioning member of society, then lying seems justified. It will save his life and others can then attempt to give him the help he needs.

What makes the case a dilemma is that any decision we make runs the risk of violating an ethical principle that we want to uphold. We want to act so as to prevent harm to others, to be trustworthy and to preserve others' freedom. Our ranking of these values and our understanding of the sort of society we wish to preserve will determine our choice. The choice is often even more difficult when the harm we evaluate is not as clear-cut as suicide, as in cases of lying to a dying client to spare him or her pain about a child's behavior or of lying to children about their parents' problems.

Consider a variation on the case of the suicidal caller. Suppose you have concluded that Costine is justified both in lying and in sending the police to the man's home, because you think these actions will prevent serious harm and are unlikely to create distrust in others. Would you, then, be justified in lying to the man if he were a patient who had been in therapy with you for two years?

This particular variation on the dilemma highlights a central confusion about social work ethics. The confusion centers on the sort of relationship one should foster between social worker and client. In the case-study, there was only a very limited relationship between the police cadet and the suicidal caller; the circumstances were such that the caller could assume that the cadet was there to prevent suicide (thus the man's fear that the call was being traced). The police cadet had certain *limited* duties and, as he said, "I have a job to do, and I did it." These circumstances with their expected results affect our evaluation of the action. Trust is not violated in the way it might be in a case where the social worker and client have an on-going relationship.

In most social work relationships, however, the nature and context of the relationship are unclear, with the result that there is confusion about its ethical demands. Social workers' contradictory responsibilities result in clients not knowing what to expect: the social worker is to be a caring and compassionate therapist while also a kind of inspector or bureaucratic manager of adequate behavior. This, at least, is the client's perception, and it is an accurate one because the social worker is in fact responsible to the society and agency, as well as to the client. The social worker, then, is not a friend, though she sometimes acts like one and is supposed to be trusted like one. She is not always an advocate, although she sometimes is. At times she is an inspector or judge. She is, in short, a professional.

The caring, expert, and bureaucratic aspects of the role are not compatible, and they thus compound the ethical dilemmas the social worker faces. These incompatibilities will be addressed more fully in the next two chapters. They figure, however, in the question of justifying manipulation, because we will have different answers about manipulation, depending on what social role is stressed (expert, friend, advocate, bureaucrat) and in what context (recreation center, hospital, welfare agency).[27] Social workers' manipulative behavior, by its deceptive nature, emphasizes the roles of expert and bureaucrat and undermines the roles of advocate and trusted helper, though this distinction has not been sufficiently recognized or discussed. The confusion about the nature of the relationship is reflected, however, in clients' distrust of social work.[28] Social workers should make the expressed goals of the relationship consistent with the kinds of influence they actually exert over clients. This will help clarify the sort of influence the social worker hopes to have and the sort of power she does in fact have.

Recommendations

Our criteria for justified coercion in social casework will depend on how we formulate our responsibilities towards others in society and how we understand the value of freedom in relation to other values. To make a decision about coercion or manipulation, five questions were suggested that can help isolate important ethical considerations:

(1) What values are violated by the coercive act?
(2) What is the good of the coercive act?
(3) Is the client competent to decide?
(4) How does the social worker's power and the institutional setting affect our evaluation?
(5) What is the overall evaluation of the above factors?

Our analysis has revealed that we need to add two more questions:

(6) What view of society do our answers reveal?
(7) What sorts of relationships do our decisions promote?

In making decisions, we need to pay particular attention to two factors.

(A) As social workers mandated to care for others, we have more power than an ordinary person who attempts to help her neighbor. The power makes the role paternal or maternal, rather than fraternal. We must be careful that our power is not misused and that we are not imposing on a powerless group of people standards which are not imposed elsewhere in the society. More generally, we need to evaluate the ethics of having this sort of power over others. This issue will be taken up again in Chapter 7.

(B) Professional values can lead us too readily to assume the incompetence of clients. Clear and precise criteria of competence need to be spelled out, in order to avoid assuming incompetence of clients who are able to make their own decisions, and in order to make clear the political assumptions of the criteria.

These two factors are connected, since often we are able to

convince ourselves and others of clients' incompetence because of their powerlessness in the society.

While overt coercion is sometimes acceptable, manipulation rarely is and always should be carefully examined. It violates a person's freedom two-fold: the freedom to choose and the freedom to know the way one is being influenced. Manipulation may be justified if some other value is of overriding importance – if, say, it is the only way to prevent catastrophe. The danger is that because it is usually covert, there is no check on the power of the worker.

Manipulation is sometimes justified from the perspectives of professional social work values: allegedly the "objectivity" and "neutrality" of the social worker's help empower the client and help him or her achieve a better life. I have argued, however, that in fact manipulation often undermines the autonomy of a client, undermines trust in the relationship, and increases the power of the social worker. This conclusion emerges if one recognizes the ethical and political nature of any sort of counseling.

The following suggestions can serve to facilitate the debate about the use of coercion and manipulation in social work practice.

(1) Agencies, and individuals in private practice as well, should develop a statement, given to all clients, which outlines basic ethical and political assumptions of the agency or individual. It should include questions clients might ask about the agency and about the individual worker, if they want more detailed information. In this way, social workers would encourage clients to take an active role and would inform them of their rights, without forcing information on them unwillingly.
(2) Criteria of informed consent should be developed, published by the agency and distributed to staff and clients. These criteria should be subject to regular evaluation by staff and clients.
(3) Agencies should institutionalize a process whereby clients and staff can register and address complaints of coercive treatment. This process should be made known to all clients and should include arbitrators from outside the agency.
(4) Agencies should give high priority in hiring to creating

diversity of staff. There is a tendency to hire "those like ourselves," but diversity in background, race, class, and point of view can facilitate real questioning and debate about agency policies and goals.

(5) Periodically, staff meetings should devote a session to discussion of coercive elements in treatment of clients and to criteria of competence. The issues will thereby be kept alive and the staff's awareness of them regularly reawakened. Such discussion should also be an established part of in-service training.

6 Dealing with bureaucracy

> [Man] should not have to wait – suffering, struggling, withering, as the case may be – while the wheels of social justice grind out social change, or, even when reform is swift, until that change makes its way through the labyrinth of policy-programme-process to affect him at weary last.[1]

> Every morning, I reach with sickening pity into this ancient object, where three rows of case histories, filed according to date and category, await decisions. Now and then they are removed, stapled to sheets of background information, refiled under new reference numbers, sent for consideration to other offices, and returned dog-eared and covered with endless scribblings. And here they lie.
> I sometimes wonder what would happen if suddenly they were to start talking. What sounds would issue from that cabinet! Children's cries, women's moans, resounding blows, quarrels, obscenities, recriminations, interrogations, hasty decisions, false testimony, administrative platitudes, jovial police slang, judges' verdicts . . . my colleagues' embittered humor, my own solitary invective, and so on and so on.[2]

Introduction

Large-scale public bureaucracies increasingly shape social work practice.[3] In these "people-changing" and "people-processing" organizations, individual social workers often seem caught up by organizational forces well beyond their control. Their work may be determined more by institutional rules than by client needs, and they often find themselves mired in routinized procedures defining a narrow range of client problems. Instead of providing "care" and empowerment, they become a force for social control or for ineffective, palliative measures.[4]

In response to these problems, social work literature focuses primarily on the need for restructuring organizations and social policies.[5] While such changes are essential, they give little guidance to the practicing social worker in her daily life within a bureaucracy: she must continue to make decisions despite inadequate resources, case overloads, excessive paper work and a labyrinth of rules, all of which contribute to a sense of helplessness and hopelessness.

Social workers rarely receive formal training about bureaucratic problems. They are often educated instead in sophisticated techniques of psychiatric casework and group work, as if they were going into practice unimpeded by organizational demands.

This chapter will focus on ethical issues within bureaucracies, *from the point of view of social workers' particular, daily decisions*. My argument is that bureaucracies, by virtue of the kind of decision-making they promote, undermine our ordinary concepts of morality. In particular, *human service* organizations undermine our moral concepts, because of their contradictory nature: their *stated* goal is to help clients, yet their actual operation serves the interest of preserving the bureaucracy. When this conflict is not recognized, workers often function as if their bureaucratic decisions do not have moral dimensions.

The most troubling problems, then, are generally those whose moral status and consequences are themselves unclear, obscured by bureaucratic structure. The chief danger is posed not so much by explicit moral challenges in organizations as by the gradual erosion of one's ethical stance day by day. While bureaucracies differ widely in terms of size, service provided, clientele, goals, etc., they are alike in many of the bureaucratic problems they create.

Rather than begin this chapter with a case-study, I will first discuss some of the ways bureaucracies erode moral responsibility. Specific cases will then be introduced to illustrate these issues. The final section will describe how social workers can begin to counteract the undermining effects of bureaucracies and work to make them morally responsive.

Bureaucracy: undermining morality

Within philosophy and the social sciences, there is an on-going debate about how bureaucracies function and whether they can be made responsive to moral problems: more and more of our lives are played out within them; if, by their nature, they elicit amoral or immoral behavior, then our lives will be increasingly dominated by such behavior.

The debate begins with the work of M. Weber who characterized bureaucracies' formal traits in terms of an ideal or rational functioning which was morally neutral – the determination of the most efficient means for achieving predetermined ends.[6] Other models of bureaucracy have since been proposed and wide variations noted.[7] I shall not focus on empirical studies but rather on ethical problems that arise for any bureaucracy, due to its structural features.[8]

A bureaucracy can be defined very generally as a "pattern of group behavior" which "describes a way in which people make group decisions, systematize and coordinate their activities, deliberate and frame projects. . . ."[9] In theory at least, bureaucratic activities have the following characteristics: (1) *Social relations are defined impersonally*: activities are organized by task or role and not primarily by ties of friendship, kinship or personal whim. (2) *Appointment and promotion are decided on the basis of merit* – merit represents what a person has earned through competence at required tasks. (3) *Work is specialized*, so that each person is engaged in some aspect of the overall work, but is usually not knowledgeable about the whole product. (4) *Authority is hierarchical*: one is expected to obey a superior, on the basis of specialized rules. (5) *And one is expected to put aside one's personal obligations to focus on one's work obligations.*[10]

These factors result in organizational standards that by their nature deviate from ordinary moral ones. Most important, they result in an absence of *moral* responsibility for actions within a bureaucracy. Moral responsibility must be distinguished from other sorts, such as role, legal, or causal responsibility. In a bureaucracy, for example, a worker is responsible for fulfilling her *role* – she is responsible for helping her clients, filling out case records, etc. She also has *legal* responsibilities – to know and obey the law. She is legally responsible for filing a child abuse report when she suspects abuse. And we can also speak of her responsibility for past actions she has performed (*causal* responsibility); we hold her accountable for cancelling the meeting. In these situations, however, the responsibility need not be moral.

Moral responsibility, by contrast, involves concern for the rightness or goodness of one's actions. Though harder to describe, it is a central concept in our lives. Goodpaster and Matthews, in an article on the morality of corporations, suggest its central aspect:

> *Respect.* The moral point of view also includes a special awareness of and concern for the effects of one's decisions and policies on others, special in the sense that it goes beyond the kind of awareness and concern that would ordinarily be part of rationality, that is, beyond seeing others merely as instrumental to accomplishing one's own purposes. This is respect for the lives of others and involves taking their needs and interests seriously, not simply as resources in one's own decision-making but as limiting conditions which change the very definition of one's habitat from a self-centered to a shared environment.[11]

While this definition is not precise, it serves to indicate the difference between moral and other sorts of responsibility. Moral responsibility is not transferable from one person to another, and it goes beyond instrumentality to consideration of one's obligations to act for the overall good of others and society – the very concerns promoted by social work ideals.

By contrast, bureaucratic decision-making is based on role and legal responsibility and actually undermines moral responsibility.

(1) Most important, organizational decisions are sharply differentiated from personal ones. An employee is expected to do particular tasks (her job description) regardless of her personal feelings or beliefs. Any decision she makes is as an instrument of the organization and for its benefit. This expectation of bureaucracies has often been characterized as a *double standard* – a split between personal and organizational life. In effect, it frees employees from the demands of their personal moralities. For example, while you might not personally like the idea of withholding a loan from a needy individual, the objectives of the bank demand it. While you might *personally* wish to give welfare recipients more money, the organization forbids it. Your personal values do not appear

violated, however, because you separate them from your work role. Being a good worker demands these decisions. You do not hold yourself *personally* responsible for the action, because the choice is made *impersonally* for the organization. Thus, in an important sense, you make decisions that are not yours. Even at the top of the hierarchy, the decision-making official is not personally responsible for decisions because supposedly she makes them solely for the good of the organization, not in terms of any other good.

The result of this split between personal and organizational morality is that an employee can dismiss general ethical considerations from evaluation of job performance. Being a good worker may mean acting unethically, but the job performance is not evaluated in these terms. No one is *morally* responsible for anything an organization does and the only applicable criteria for evaluating work are the organizational objectives themselves.

(2) Further, because the stated goals are often viewed as predetermined and not debatable, the only area of decision-making is how best to achieve the goals. The best way is often translated as the *most efficient* way: a technical, rather than an ethical matter. For example, in a factory you may be required to make a lower quality product, because it saves the company time and money. In human services, you may be urged to place a child in a foster home rather than a residential treatment school, because the more expensive treatment plan is viewed as "inefficient" and "costly." This allegedly rational decision-making process, however, often runs counter to our notions of moral agency and moral responsibility, which involve full consideration of the choices and their effects, based on the overall "good" to society.

(3) Other features of bureaucratic decision-making further contribute to undermining moral responsibility. Workers are usually specialized and therefore responsible for only part of a product and not the product as a whole. If you work on the assembly line of a coal manufacturing plant you do not take responsibility for the polluted atmosphere that the factory produces. If you are the intake worker in a child welfare agency you do not take responsibility for what others do with your information. This specialized division of labor encourages

workers to look only at their work and not at its integration or implications. Again, individual moral responsibility is undermined.

(4) In addition, decision-making is usually hierarchical in nature and bound by rules. Decisions you make are not fully your own but determined by rules and goals of the organization, your supervisor, or a case conference for which no one person takes responsibility. Workers are encouraged to accept such authority and not to question it.

(5) At least one other factor operates in bureaucracies to undermine our moral agency. The "official" language serves to obscure the ethical dimensions of our decisions. It pictures a technical world, a world of products, profits, and specialized knowledge, but one surprisingly devoid of ordinary human interaction.

People become "cases," ending a relationship becomes "closing a case," family tragedies become "crisis management," and so on. The bureaucratized language often masks what really goes on. As Lipsky points out, many verbs have been turned into nouns, obscuring what is being done to whom. We refer to levels of "care," without specifying who cares about what, thereby obscuring our goals.[12] When a rule is disregarded, we may refer to the action as a "special case" or "exception," without fully confronting or questioning the implications of the rule.

Certain particularly distasteful tasks, which may even comprise the bulk of our work, may be designated as "dirty work" to indicate that it is not our real or serious work. Consider, for example, the work of the psychiatric emergency team (PET) at a Southern California mental health clinic:

> if one observed PET activities in the absence of worker's [sic] running commentary on their work, one might reasonably conclude that PET'S most significant function served not therapeutic but social control purposes. After all, day after day PET hospitalized people who did not want to be hospitalized, used coercion in effecting hospitalization, and so forth. By contrast, through the "narration" provided both in general talk of PET as shit work and in identifying particular work tasks as shit work . . . PET personnel made

> themselves and others aware that the actual treatment accorded cases ought not to be taken as representative of what they would prefer to do or what PET, at heart, was designed to do.[13]

Social work frequently involves distasteful tasks and inadequate or shoddy treatment of clients. We tend to focus instead on our successful cases or on the kind of treatment we would like to be able to give all the time: sometimes we must act this way to avoid "burn-out." The danger, however, is that we may not take moral responsibility for large areas of our work, because we have designated those areas as peripheral. The "sanitized" language in human service bureaucracies increases the danger of our doing so.

On many levels, then, our use of language in bureaucracies serves to reinforce acceptance of bureaucratic standards as the sole arbiters of organizational morality.

Working in a bureaucracy may create for us a kind of "moral schizophrenia" or "double life;" we compartmentalize our decisions and let the organizational standards take over:

> the individual's own decisions and actions become separated from himself as a person and become the decisions and actions of another, e.g. of an organization. They become social decisions, not decisions of the individual. . . .
>
> . . . As his actions are turned into social decisions, the individual is alienated from them and is *eo ipso* alienated from other men and from morality. In adopting the administrator's point of view (or that of a utilitarian) and so losing his actions, the individual becomes dehumanized and demoralized. For morality is essentially a relation between men, as individuals, and in losing this relation, one loses morality itself.[14]

We are asked to become our roles as good bureaucrats, but in doing so we run the risk of giving up our moral selves.

Human service bureaucracies

The question remains: do bureaucracies necessarily and inevitably undermine their employees' moral responsibility? Can they be modified to allow for moral responsibility, both of their employees and of the bureaucracies themselves?

The ideal human service bureaucracy seemingly combines the best features of bureaucracies without sacrificing the ethical dimension of our lives: it aims to promote mass treatment of clients in an equitable, efficient way, with humane concern for the unique needs of each client. Because human service employees have professional status, with some discretion over decision-making, they are not closely supervised and act on their expertise rather than on a given set of rules. They have direct contact with people and are supposed to care about them and be their advocates, none of which fits the bureaucratic aim of employee impersonality. Thus, it seems that human service bureaucracies will have less hold over their employees and that employees will have more control over, and responsibility for, their decisions. As Prottas states:

> For some tasks street-level bureaucracies are the best tool at hand. . . . We seek regularity and consistency because our sense of justice demands it. We seek the exercise of human judgment because the problems confronted and the people encountered cannot be met with rote formulas. In essence we seek two incompatible goals, a contradiction that reflects our entirely proper desire that each should moderate the other.[15]

In fact, however, the contradictions between the individualized, caring concern of a social worker and bureaucracies' impersonal requirements do not result in more humane organizations.[16] On the contrary, these organizations are in some ways the most harmful of all because of their false promise of caring concern. Bureaucratic impersonality takes over and transforms human service ideals to fit its own purposes: work is still specialized, directed by rules, evaluated hierarchically and assessed for efficiency and productivity. These factors serve to undermine goals of empowering clients, of treating them with respect and dignity, of "caring" about them. Let us examine how this occurs.

(1) *Specialization* – Although work is specialized to provide the most knowledgeable and efficient service to clients, it often results in making both workers and clients feel helpless and depersonalized instead. A client's problems are divided among

several workers (intake, day program, medical care) and agencies (family service, welfare, school counseling): clients thus feel divided up into bureaucratic pieces and have the confusing task of figuring out who should do what. Similarly, a worker is involved with only a piece of the problem, and may feel helpless to effect change in the client's overall plan. Workers and agencies may spend considerable time and energy denying their responsibility for a case – each is only responsible for a piece of it – with the result that no one will take primary responsibility.

With specialization, case records take on increased importance, as they – or a hurried conversation with a worker involved with some piece of a case – may provide a worker's chief understanding of a client. Case records may largely determine how we perceive a client, yet they are designed to give a quick evaluation. "It is not that records record things but that the very idea of recording determines in advance how things will have to appear."[17] Workers may come to view clients in terms of categories on forms and clients often view themselves similarly: "An important part of this process is the way people learn to treat themselves as if they were categorical entities."[18] Bureaucratic aims of efficiency are served by this sort of "management," but in the process we may lose our original goals of bettering the lives of clients; both clients and workers feel depersonalized and have difficulty relating to each other.

(2) *Rules and regulations* – Rules and regulations, designed to simplify and ensure equitable service, often serve instead to alienate workers and clients.

Rules can never cover all the situations social workers confront. In addition, rules may be so numerous, conflicting, and changeable that they must be followed selectively. Social workers therefore still have to use discretion in deciding whether and how rules apply, and their own values inevitably play a part in this process. For example, workers will vary, among themselves and towards different clients, in the extent to which they make clients aware of benefits or special programs. Rules thus do not eliminate bias. Instead they often serve both to mask the real and different value-judgments workers make and to confuse clients who do not know how the rules will be interpreted.[19] Thus, value-judgments usually remain unexamined and clients may end up feeling unempowered and depersonalized, rather than equitably and efficiently treated according to the ideal.[20]

(3) *Hierarchical decision-making* – Most damaging of all, the rules take on a life of their own. Instead of being a means to achieving good service, they become the end itself. Workers are encouraged to focus on rules, regulations, and paper work, but not to think beyond them. The rules in effect become policy.[21] The point is nicely made by a mid-level administrator of welfare in Massachusetts:

> You must not forget that we are all bureaucrats, and most of us accept the rules of the bureaucracy. We know we need to carry out the federal and state rules so we don't think to question them. . . .
>
> During the time you are talking about [1966–78] a lot of people liked the rules from Washington so it seemed OK to you to follow them. But that wasn't why people in Welfare went along, we went along because it was our job and would have gone along with other rules if we had to. Don't fool yourself.[22]

The overall procedures of an agency, however undesirable, can become "givens" which are unquestioned after the first few months. One becomes used to following the rules and accepting supervisors' suggestions. Time demands are such that there isn't extra time to reflect quietly on what one is doing. In this area, particularly, our moral questioning can be eroded without our even realizing it.

(4) *Evaluation procedures* – Evaluation procedures ironically further undermine human service goals. Since bureaucracies do not know how best to evaluate *quality* of service, they often rely instead on what can more easily be evaluated: efficiency and productivity. They measure productivity by such factors as volume of service and case closings, even though such factors bear little relation to good service. Whereas an evaluation procedure should be a means to safeguard human service goals, it in effect replaces them.

Efficiency and productivity become the real goals and often conflict with goals of caring for and helping others.

Programs are also frequently evaluated in terms of their ability to bring new funds into an agency. If a program does not generate funds, or is not in current political favor, then even if it provides better service to clients than other programs, it may be phased out. Again, agency interests tend to predominate over concern for the client.

This process sometimes also occurs in an odd way in the relationships of social workers to clients. Social work is supposed to encourage relationships in which the social worker genuinely cares about the client. Under the pressure of time and scarce resources, a social worker may "care about" a client chiefly as a means to bring about some other end, such as closing the case or persuading the client of some course of action. This distortion of "caring" will be discussed more fully in the next chapter.

Most significant of all, most agencies never ask clients to evaluate their services in any way, and the social work literature on client evaluation is still sparse. Again, clients are made to feel in practice that their opinions are not of much significance. It is ironic that clients are considered the least important evaluators of whether they have received help and whether their autonomy and dignity have been respected.

In all the ways mentioned, bureaucratic structure operates steadily to direct workers to be responsive to their agency rather than to clients. The myth persists, however, that the discretionary, professional judgment of the worker results in humane and responsive attention to individual needs. The harmful effects of bureaucracies are thus obscured and not readily apparent to workers, clients or the public.

For example, public agencies can stress their stated goal of meeting the basic needs of recipients, adding that these needs must be assessed using the expert evaluations of their social workers. In fact, as we have seen, the stated goal is often replaced by an operative goal – enacted through procedural rules – of limiting help as much as possible. The operative goals, however, may remain unquestioned, because the public and social workers themselves buy into the notion that workers are determining the needy on the basis of their discretion.[23]

Put another way, "discretion" is often used to fudge conflicting purposes embodied in legislation and administrative directives. A compromise of sorts is reached by simply leaving the issue to the discretion of social workers. In this way, the conflict is not made explicit and is therefore less apt to be confronted and resolved. "Discretion can prevent the coalescing of open issues around which political struggle can take place."[24]

It might be argued that the moral failings of human service organizations do not result from bureaucratic structure but from inadequate resources combined with increased demand. Certainly in this decade of new cutbacks to social programs and higher case loads characteristics like impersonality of work and objectification of client are magnified. These bureaucratic features, however, characterize human services whatever the political climate and are basic to bureaucracies as they are currently structured.

Thus, human service organizations turn out to have the same undesirable characteristics as other bureaucracies: they discourage workers from questioning rules, goals, methods of evaluation or inconsistencies in the organization, thereby discouraging them from questioning the nature of the services they provide. Workers, who are to remain morally detached, divide the client into pieces which are to be efficiently handled. The professional role of discretion, then, instead of serving clients' best interests, serves more often to mask bureaucratic features.

Once we understand how bureaucracies erode our moral stands, we can examine our bureaucratic decisions more closely, to see what values we act on and what alternatives we have.

Case-studies

Two cases will be presented. The first raises issues about *whistle-blowing on colleagues*. This issue embodies important, explicit value conflicts; and its usual resolution erodes morality. The second case highlights the conflict between *helping a client* and *obeying an agency's rules*.

Case: Joe

> You are a social worker in a large mental health agency. A client, Ellen, is transferred to you from another worker, Joe, who is taking on some administrative tasks in addition to casework. Ellen is a severely depressed twenty-six-year-old who has been in treatment for a year and a half. She was referred to the agency while on probation for a shoplifting conviction. At that time her daughter appeared neglected. Ellen agreed to a temporary foster home placement but wants to take her daughter back soon.

Suppose that after seeing Ellen for a few months you discover the following:

(1) In discussing the case with Joe, you realize that he is an alcoholic, confused and vague about the case.
(2) Ellen tells you that Joe made sexual advances to her; she convinces you that she is telling the truth.
(3) Ellen has been put on a drug, recommended by Joe and prescribed by the agency's psychiatrist, which you consider grossly inappropriate as a treatment modality for her.
(4) Although Joe told you that he was seeing Ellen once a week, he continually broke appointments and saw her approximately once a month.

What should you do? What are the relevant ethical factors?

Joe's alcoholism or sexual misconduct may seem extreme illustrations, but unfortunately they are more common than we might want to suppose.[25] Neither expresses a moral dilemma: Joe's conduct clearly violates the ethics of the profession, agency, and society, and endangers the client. The moral problem centers not on deciding between competing moral principles but on figuring out a viable course of action. Too often we feel outraged by such cases but feel helpless to do anything about them.

When we must choose between believing a client or colleague, we frequently dismiss the client's point of view. This attitude suggests that *in practice* we feel more accountable to colleagues than to clients. Even in cases where we know from multiple reports that a colleague is misbehaving, clients' reports are ignored. This is not really surprising. We have to live with our colleagues, not usually our clients, and tend to feel more comfortable with them, in terms of values, class background, work experience. We feel "disloyal" reporting a colleague's misconduct. In addition, as fellow workers, we do not have the authority to discipline colleagues and usually do not want to hurt their careers. If a co-worker supervises us and we report her, we may also risk losing our jobs.

The moral problem arises, then, not in deciding that something must be done but rather in figuring out what *can* be done. In theory, you would talk to Joe and then if necessary report him to your supervisor or the appropriate disciplinary board. In practice, however, you may know that nothing will be done with your report, particularly if Joe is well-liked or well-established. The result may simply be your ostracism within the agency and the continued misconduct of your colleague. Workers thus tend to complain privately among themselves about such misconduct but take no action.

This sort of non-resolution illustrates the ways in which bureaucratric structure subtly operates to discourage workers from moral action. A worker is encouraged to focus on her own work, only to evaluate others' work if she is their supervisor, and to obey the directives of her agency. If she has complaints they should be directed to the relevant supervisors, who in turn have their own supervisors. There is thus no explicit accountability of colleagues to each other. In a field that values self-evaluation, colleagues are in fact discouraged from questioning their own behavior or that of others.

This hierarchical system also encourages workers to believe that their moral responsibility can be transferred to another person. For example, once you have told your supervisor about Joe you are no longer in any way responsible for his misconduct, according to this bureaucratic reasoning, even if you know that no action will be taken. You have given that responsibility to your supervisor. Moral responsibility, however, unlike other sorts of responsibility, is concern for the good of others and of society. If you believe that you are morally responsible for a particular situation – for example, for revealing the unethical conduct of a colleague – then you do not rid yourself of that responsibility by placing it on another person when you expect nothing to be done. That other person may *also* become responsible, but your responsibility remains.

The most dramatic and grotesque illustrations of this idea come from Nazi Germany, where, for example, some Nazi officers claimed after the War that they did not personally act against Jews. Since the actual killing was carried out by co-workers and ordered by supervisors, the officers claimed that they were not morally responsible. While this illustration is extreme, it serves to show how bureaucratric structure can blunt our moral sense.[26]

When confronted with Joe's alcoholism or sexual misconduct, we are encouraged simply to report it to our supervisor and to believe that we thereby fulfill our moral responsibility. If nothing is done we can tell ourselves that there is nothing else we can do, or we refrain from investigating further in order to believe that maybe something has changed, contrary to appearances. This pattern is responsible for much of the alienation and cynicism of workers about the moral dimensions of their work. It is evident in the following quote from a human service worker:

> The woman I reported is still on the same ward. . . . Would I do it again – yes. If you had asked me a year ago I may have said no. It definitely shook my faith in justice and in my ability to change things.[27]

What more, then, can we say about this sort of case? What ought we to do, when faced with an incompetent co-worker?

Let us consider five alternative courses of action: a worker might (1) try to organize other workers jointly to take action; (2) go to the union, if there is one; (3) try to organize clients to take action; (4) make everyone in the agency aware of the misconduct and thereby indirectly pressure the worker to change; (5) go to the public, through media coverage, legislative hearings, etc.

(1) Organizing other workers to take action, if successful, is more apt to result in a real change than acting alone. This alternative, however, reveals how much human service work is organized hierarchically, isolating workers from each other. Workers are usually reluctant to organize and often regard

organizing as "unprofessional" and "political," as well as a threat to their own jobs, particularly when action is being urged against a supervisor.[28]

(2) Going to the union should be another way to organize fellow workers, but often unions are reluctant to get involved, or they act to protect individual workers from just such actions. In spite of these problems, this course of action can help workers break down their isolation from each other, to open up discussion of moral issues, and to make unions more receptive to client demands.[29]

(3) Organizing clients to take action is considered even more suspect. It is viewed as unprofessional because it explicitly brings personal and political values into service work (as if they were not already there) and allegedly involves using clients for one's own purposes. This sort of response reveals how human service workers consider themselves more accountable to the agency and each other than to their clients. Even though Joe may be seriously damaging clients, fellow workers may refrain from warning clients or urging them to take action. We must question this attitude, if we are serious in our aim of empowering and helping clients.[30]

That client evaluations of service work are rarely sought and almost always ignored illustrates how much these entrenched procedures govern social work practice.

(4) Exposing or pressuring the worker, the fourth alternative, appears to be a viable response, particularly after attempts to resolve the issue through formal channels have failed. Two problems arise, however, if we choose this alternative: first, since the worker has no structured avenue through which to defend herself, she will have been denied due process. That, in itself, raises ethical questions. Second, even if successful, this alternative does nothing to challenge the basic structure, which discourages workers from taking full moral responsibility for their work.

(5) The final alternative, going public, has usually been considered a last resort. Workers usually reserve this approach for the most flagrant abuses, such as larceny, widespread client abuse, or gross administrative incompetence. Even then, a worker should be certain that formal procedures have failed, so that she does not risk undermining the agency's and her own effectiveness.

Quietly approaching a segment of the community, however, may provide a viable option, particularly when all else has failed; in alerting those most concerned, a worker can empower herself, involve the community ostensibly being served, and leave open the possibility for due process with the community group as watchdog.

So far, we have considered two situations of flagrantly unethical conduct by a co-worker or supervisor. What of more common and problematical situations? What if you discover that a colleague or a supervisor is simply sloppy or lazy or uses techniques you believe to be inappropriate?

If, for example, a co-worker constantly breaks appointments and lies about it, we may respond by thinking it is "not our business" to do anything. Particularly if no dramtic injury is done to clients, we can overlook the more subtle kind of harm that comes from cancelled appointments, inadequate treatment plans, poor referral service, etc. Besides, this sort of misconduct is hard to document, when even the most diligent human service workers give inadequate service because of limited time and resources. Over a period of time, though, inattention to detail may do significant harm to clients, as well as undermine the work of our colleagues, if we do not confront these situations explicitly.

Finally, consider the situation of a worker using techniques which you believe to be unethical but which are tacitly or explicitly approved by the agency. In the example given, Joe puts Ellen on medication which you think she does not need. Another worker may use aversive behavior modification techniques which you find unethical. A third worker may have started a group without adequate supervision or may be too rigid in determining client need "by the rules." What should you do?

Too often workers and supervisors subscribe to a myth of agreed-upon goals and techniques, when in fact they disagree strongly about services. Case conferences are supposed to be forums for expressing and resolving some of these differences, but often they serve instead as a show piece for visiting consultants or as a public exhibition of a worker's best case. Thus, if you believe that an agency has been prescribing inappropriate medication, you may find it difficult to have the agency address this practice. The issue is not regarded as yours. At best, you may be able to have Ellen's case reconsidered, if it is now your case. But if Joe is still in charge, there may be no forum for discussing the value differences.

One solution to this sort of problem is to make case conferences and staff meetings real forums for openly discussing value differences. This would of course imply a significant change in the structure of most agencies, with more participation from co-workers and less authority flowing from policy to supervisor to worker.

Again, the solutions suggested for the extreme cases are relevant here as well. To protest inappropriate treatment, you may try to bring the issue to the attention of other workers, clients, or the public. Within agencies, we need to develop and institutionalize ways to discuss differences in our clinical practices and views.

In the next case, we shall examine in more depth the ethical issues presented by conflicting worker views. While worker disagreement centered on treatment issues in Joe's case, it centers on political issues in the next one.

Case

> You are a social worker in a large public agency that provides social services to mothers with dependent children. New regulations are instituted, based on recently passed legislation, requiring mothers who receive financial aid to register for work and to accept any job for which they qualify (known as Workfare). You know that the available jobs are unskilled, that they pay clients no more than they now receive, and that they necessitate the mothers' absence from home many hours a day.
>
> Suppose that you believe these regulations are unethical, because they deny poor women the opportunity to stay at home with their children, provide inadequate job training and result in women accepting jobs at low pay, which undermines union efforts to upgrade work.
>
> What should you do?

In this situation your personal values directly conflict with rules you are required to enforce. While Workfare may be a clear-cut example of value conflict, there are many others which illustrate how often and how much workers are expected to put aside personal convictions.

> New rules and regulations may require that you terminate rehabilitative services to a client who needs them, that you place a child inappropriately in a mental hospital because no other placement is available, that you use a foster home which you know to be inadequate, or that you deny welfare benefits to a hungry client because she has no address.

In some of these situations workers will disagree among themselves about which rules are unethical. As one worker stated about food stamps:

> There are two different kinds of people at my office. Some of us think that people without money have a right to food stamps and that our job is to help them get as much as they are eligible for. Some other people seem to think that people should be grateful for whatever they get and that our job is to make sure we don't give anybody any more than they absolutely need. It's funny, but it makes a big difference how you look at it, even though none of us are trying to break the rules.[31]

Workfare is also a particularly good example of this sort of conflict. Some workers may believe that the regulation is a good one, that it will reduce welfare costs and numbers and will provide meaningful work, while others believe it promotes slave labor.

Resolving these dilemmas becomes difficult because they embody unexpressed ethical and political conflicts in the society. Workfare is justified from some political viewpoints and not from others. Your point of view will depend on your beliefs about what society owes to its members – is there a right to welfare? Are we obligated to care for the children of others? What constitutes equal opportunities for poor women?

These conflicts are often not explicitly recognized by agencies, which operate as if they uphold coherent sets of goals, nor recognized by workers who themselves differ on the appropriate goals of the agency.

If we return to our case, you as the worker may believe that requiring Workfare is unethical. You cannot assume, however, that other workers or the public will agree with you. Although you are encouraged to believe that you are simply the implementer of a policy that was democratically decided at a higher level of legislative action, you know that at the higher level many of the realities of human service needs were not taken into account and that a full debate about social priorities never took place. You believe that the public, legislators and the agency are, in effect, ignoring their paradoxical policy and have not examined the implications of the laws and rules they promulgate.

What, then, should you do?

If you refuse outright to implement the new policy, you risk losing your job without affecting any change. Your success in opposing a policy will depend on its importance, the views of your supervisors (and perhaps co-workers) and the way you oppose it. Sometimes workers can violate rules frequently and quietly, and doing so becomes accepted informal policy. In extreme cases, such as the hungry client who has no address, violation of the rule may be the only effective solution available in time.

Its dangers, however, are two-fold: (1) It encourages workers to act independently of the rules and thus perhaps in arbitrary and unjust ways towards clients. While such disregard of the rules may result in more ethical treatment of a client, it may just as easily result in punitive and unwarranted treatment. (2) If you do not explicitly confront the rule, you are in the position of giving it tacit support: others will continue to act on it; you may act on it with other clients; and you are part of a system that accepts it.

With a highly political regulation like Workfare, quiet disregard of the rule may not be possible in any case. There are several options a worker might consider: (1) organizing other workers to violate the rule; (2) organizing clients; (3) getting the union to take action; or (4) going with other workers and clients to legislators or the media to focus attention on the issue. These actions, however, are usually rejected because they are seen as violating agency policies and sometimes as violating professional social work norms.

Anything a worker does or fails to do in this sort of case, however, will be political. Workfare itself is political. It involves assumptions about social priorities, about "deserving" and "undeserving" poor, about the role of poor women in society, and so on. Whatever a worker decides, she takes a political stand on the issue. Only if this stand is made explicit does it become clear that workers disagree about goals and procedures and that the agency itself does not have coherent goals. Debate will become possible. Speaking out is essential.

While speaking out may appear to be futile or ineffective, its importance should not be underestimated. It breaks the pattern of resignedly carrying out agency rules. We can initiate real discussion of the issues among workers, supervisors and clients. The agency or legislature will not then be able so easily to cover over inconsistencies with generalities about service goals. And we can begin to connect our professional responsibilities to our personal moralities. Most important, we can break the alienation that results from believing that nothing can be done.

Proposals

Bureaucratic norms tend to undermine moral responsibility in a variety of ways: workers are encouraged to do their specialized clinical work and to follow agency rules without questioning inconsistencies or the underpinnings of their actions. They are encouraged to put aside personal commitments and operate under the illusion that agency rules and professional norms embody the best course of action.

Moral responsibility is also undermined by the staggering demands of the work: ethical issues arise constantly, but lack of time and resources means that workers must act immediately and then move on to the next problem. The work, in effect, becomes a problem of management – how to get through a caseload – and the ethical issues get lost in the shuffle.

When workers are faced with an unavoidable ethical problem, such as the hungry client with no address who does not qualify for help or an incompetent supervisor, often the action taken is an isolated one, such as making an exception or filing a complaint about which nothing is done. There is a sense that nothing can be done and this in turn contributes to the frustration, alienation and demoralization of workers.

To encourage moral responsibility in bureaucracies, we need a new approach – an approach which would in effect begin to *debureaucratize* bureaucracies.

Workers must begin to break down the radical separation between their personal integrity and their professional lives, by accepting responsibility for the ethical and political dimensions of their work. If they do so, then they will of necessity have to respond differently to their agency, clients, and community:

(1) Workers should speak out, making clear the politics behind alternative courses of action and pointing out inconsistencies in their agency's operation.
(2) They should form alliances with other workers and with clients to bring pressure to bear on policy issues.
(3) They should begin to question rules and regulations, rather than simply make exceptions as best they can.
(4) They should act as lobbyists – offering their expertise on legislative committees, pushing for legislative action, and informing the public about human service issues.

Some of these strategies are partially employed by the N.A.S.W. which has political action groups that lobby for increased funds for human services. The N.A.S.W. however, usually lobbies to increase services within existing bureaucratic structures, without making explicit its underlying political and ethical assumptions.[32] Strategies that involve organizing clients are often identified exclusively with "radical" social work – that is, with a perspective which views current social services as sustaining a capitalist economic system which must be replaced by socialism in order to empower clients.

My chief point spans both these perspectives. If social workers are to be moral agents in bureaucratic settings, then speaking out, questioning, and forming alliances with other workers and clients is necessary. The sorts of alliances will reflect different political and ethical assumptions.

Second, if social workers take seriously a goal of "empowering" clients, then their commitments cannot be simply to the bureaucracy, with its conflicting agendas and its tendencies to undermine human service goals. As the cases illustrate, bureaucratic structure encourages empowerment of the bureaucracy rather than of the client. This inconsistency should be made explicit and this will only happen if workers speak out.

While the approach recommended here will undermine traditional bureaucratic organization, my point is that we need to search for new forms of management which allow for individual moral responsibility and for full debate of the issues. The conflicting responsibilities of workers within an agency – to provide "good" service, empower clients, save money, be efficient – with their differing ethical underpinnings reveal clearly that individuals in a bureaucracy do not constitute a community of shared interests. By making the conflicts explicit, however, it may be possible to begin to define different interests and to create new forms of decision-making.[33]

None of these proposals is made lightly. Any sort of change within a bureaucracy is difficult to make. Even when action is carefully and persistently pursued, it may appear to lead nowhere. It takes time, and you risk job security and promotions, unless you have a solid base of support among workers or in the community.

At some point a worker may be faced with a related moral issue: "Given the unethical practices I must engage in should I continue to work for change from within or should I leave the agency?" "Have I become part of the problem or can I make a difference?"

These questions are troubling ones which pose opportunities for self-deception. When we examine in retrospect obvious cases of unethical behavior the answer seems clear and simple. In practice, however, it is never simple or clear: we are too personally invested in our work to see clearly. We may gradually become accustomed to practices we consider unacceptable, or we may not recognize real changes we have helped to bring about.

No general answer to this problem is possible. Simply being responsive to the issue is itself a safeguard against continuing in an untenable situation. Making one's concerns known to others in the agency and to outsiders can also help in evaluating the impact one is having. In addition, formulating agency rules and goals in terms of their ethical and political implications can help to clarify the nature of one's work and its desirability.

Some agencies have created jobs with the explicit purpose of raising ethical issues. For example, "ethicists" have been hired by prisons; social workers are hired by business corporations to help employees with adjustments; hospitals are beginning to hire "philosophers in residence." The danger of these new jobs is that moral concern becomes the province of a few expert persons (that is your job) and not truly the concern of everyone in the agency. These jobs may also function primarily to absolve management of moral responsibility and to blame workers. In such cases, the ethical issues are not really addressed, and in addition those in the agency, including the new ethicist or social worker, may be lulled into believing that some real change is taking place. The person may be able to make a difference, but only if she is aware of the dangers and makes certain that the organization does not make her its excuse for avoiding ethical issues.

Finally, I would like to stress again the importance of speaking out – of making the implicit explicit, even though this is a difficult task that sometimes appears ineffective.

Speaking out is in itself a skill that should be carefully developed. If a worker speaks out on any and every issue and becomes identified as a "trouble-maker," then speaking out will become a futile gesture. As much planning and thought should go into speaking out as goes into the most carefully planned case presentation. By thoughtfully raising questions and connecting with others who are willing to speak out, a worker can make it impossible for the ethical issues to be denied. Workers often give up on this approach because it is slow, frustrating, and its results sometimes painfully meager. It may, however, yield unseen results – new awareness on the part of other workers, repercussions in the agency after a worker has left, etc. Besides, the alternative to such action is often to do nothing at all. As two workers put it:

> We staff got together and said that something had to be done about the overcrowding which was making it impossible to

work. We threatened to go to the press. Somehow some clients were transferred and some new space was "found."

I don't know what else to do. The programs are still bad, people are still hurting, and the rules are still unfair. But I won't give them the satisfaction of thinking they have won. In my [mental health] clinic, they have to deal with me. I've been there too long and I've got too many contacts in the community. Sometimes we've even been able to stop the worst plans for our area. And when we didn't win, we didn't lose as bad as we would have if nobody opposed them.[34]

7 Creating empathy and doing good

"Impassive, draped in condescending superiority, he has the client – that frail, flustered being who wants something or is afraid of something – admitted. If the official had cares of his own, he himself would degenerate into a client in some other office, on the other side of just such a desk. The standard desk is no more than a yard deep. But the persons facing each other across it are as far apart as convict and jailer on opposite sides of the bars. There is no way round or across this desk; it stands between two faces, two enigmas, inert, but apportioning the roles as unmistakably as a whipping post or a guillotine.[1]

She intervened in the lives of the poor by virtue of a presumptive wisdom and superiority, yet was to conceive of her charges as personal friends.[2]

We hate what we are dependent upon. We become disgusted with what depends on us.[3]

Cases

From our first experiences of casework, the perplexing worker-client relationship confronts us: can I be "a friend" to my client and still be "a professional"? Can I be the client's advocate and still follow the dictates of the agency, act on my professional training, and promote the good of society?

The question of what the worker-client relationship should be underlies all of the ethical issues examined thus far. Further, it encompasses fundamental ethical themes in social work – the nature of altruism and the desirability of professional altruism. Through examining worker-client relationships, then, I shall attempt to bring together conflicts explored in earlier chapters and to make some recommendations for practice.

Let us begin, however, with the particular dilemmas faced by social workers as they try to make sense of their relationships with clients. Consider again a case described in Chapter 4 (pages 87–8).

> You are a white, middle-class, college-educated social worker, and your client, Maria, is a Chicana woman, aged twenty-four, who has recently moved to the city from a poor rural community in Mexico with her husband and two children, aged four and two. Maria was referred by her priest because she has been very depressed. She has frequent crying spells and has trouble taking any interest in her children. Her husband works long hours and they live in a three-room apartment in a large building. She does not see any point in going to a social worker and feels ashamed of it. Her husband does not like the idea but gave his approval because the priest suggested it and because his wife is unhappy but he refuses to see the social worker himself.

What sort of relationship should you try to establish with Maria? The social work literature emphasizes that in order to help her you must gain her trust and acceptance by conveying qualities of caring, warmth and empathy. Suppose that you do so through providing concrete help – arranging day-care, telling Maria how to get food stamps, taking her to a doctor – and in addition you provide regular counseling. Suppose further that Maria interprets your help as signs of "friendship." Suppose she:

(1) asks you to come for lunch on a regular basis or to attend a family party;
(2) brings you a small gift every week;
(3) asks you detailed questions about your family;
(4) wants to remain in contact after the case is closed.

What should you do? What sort of relationship can you establish that is honest, respectful, and empowering to Maria?

Consider a second case: the relationship is between a client on welfare and her social service worker.

> Alice is a twenty-six-year-old mother, with children aged four and two, whose husband left her a year ago and disappeared. Since Alice has no means of support and poor prospects for any job that would support both her family and day-care expenses, she applied for welfare, which she has

> been receiving for several months. Her youngest child has been sick for the past month with an undiagnosed ailment. Doctors are reluctant to treat her because the family is on medicaid. Alice has no place to leave her older daughter when she takes the younger one to the doctors and finds it impossible to live on her welfare allotment. She seeks the social worker's help in solving these problems.

In this case, the worker as helper and inspector has considerable power over the client, but the limits of the relationship are not clearly defined.

(1) Is the worker willing to go to her supervisor and make a case for special services for this client?
(2) Is she able and willing to see her client at a moment's notice in an emergency?
(3) Is she willing to keep in confidence evidence that the client is violating welfare regulations – as by holding a part-time job?
(4) What sort of advocacy and trust is the worker conveying? What should she convey?

To answer these questions, let us examine the recommendations of social work educators and the actual experiences of workers and clients.

Worker-client conflicts

Casework practice promotes a certain kind of relationship: the expression of care, genuineness and warmth towards the client for the purpose of affecting change.[4]

> Casework refers to a social worker's art of trying to use his relationship with people whom he assumes to be under stress, in order to mobilize their capacities and resources in their environment to reduce or solve conditions leading to such stress.[5]

The central component of this ideology is "the assumption that certain people could and should be helped through the medium of interpersonal relationships."[6] The relationship between worker and client is the heart of casework, as Perlman states, and questions about the nature of the relationship are to be settled by an understanding of proper professional techniques:

> it is part of the *skill and professional responsibility* of the helping persons to know what a helpful relationship consists of, what its components are thought to be, and to incorporate them consciously, insofar as that is possible, into his dealings with people . . .
>
> The relationship attributes that experienced clinicians (psychologists, professional social workers, psychiatrists) seem to agree upon as desirable or even necessary are these: warmth, acceptance, empathy, caring-concern, genuineness.[7]

Professional technique, however, dictates that caring must be carefully controlled. The social worker must use her warmth and empathy solely for the purpose of helping. In theory at least, she creates a time-bound relationship for the client's benefit and controls its development through objective assessment of the client's needs and potentials, including the use the client will make of particular "friendly" gestures. As Halmos states, the social worker must maintain a "keenly interested neutrality," "a non-involved involvement."[8] The involvement must be closely monitored by the social worker so as to meet the particular goals of casework.

This description of a worker's relationship to a client, however, does not adequately address the full reality of the relationship as it is experienced, a reality which forms a striking and disturbing contrast to the glowing or clear-cut descriptions found in textbooks.

Consider some clients' comments drawn from studies of worker-client relationships:

> I wondered why he was coming. . . . When he comes it's embarrassing because he doesn't seem to know what to say. . . . It seems ungrateful for me to say this but actually none of them seems able to do very much.[9]

> He didn't seem so warm. He gave you the impression that it was just his job, and he wasn't really interested.[10]

> I can't explain it, I felt like it just fell on deaf ears. Do you

> understand what I mean? I felt like it from the start, after the first interview. I felt, well it's just no good.[11]

> They make you feel frightened, they shout at you, they threaten you . . . they make you feel as if you're a nobody – they make you feel like scruff . . .[12] (regarding statutory services)

> I'm not sure I want to be a regular "social worker." All the social workers I know – and I've known plenty in my day – are pretty cold and uninvolved and act like they are better than you are – especially if you are an alcoholic.[13] (from a client who is becoming a social worker)

And from workers:

> I think a lot of clients are very demanding and manipulators and you need to watch this. Some of them would have you running every minute of the day and you have to make sure you don't fall into this trap.[14]

> I object to the ones who sort of very aggressively expect you to do something for them . . .[15]

> I was starting to hate people for wanting things, for coming to us with the same stories when we couldn't really help.[16]

One client organizer gave an even more dramatic illustration of the tensions between clients and workers:

> Last summer on Cape Cod, something happened which makes me hesitate to build alliances with workers, no matter how "correct" that strategy is. We were fighting for summer housing, always a problem on the Cape. While we were outside demonstrating, welfare workers were ordered to guard the door against us. They did. A scuffle occurred and there was fighting between some welfare social workers and some clients. So the next thing we know we were all in court charging each other with assault. How's that for class solidarity?[17]

Instead of empathy, caring, and warm regard, we find bewilderment, antagonism, and hopelessness. Pearson graphically conveys a similar public perception of social work:

> In another political cartoon of the period two "slum kids" hold a conversation: "We've got rats," says one; the other replies: "Shit man – we've got social workers."[18]

These perceptions, if accurate, raise important questions about worker-client relationships. Is this distrust and antagonism the result of social workers' inadequate skill, or is it inevitable because of the structure of the relationship? How should we understand these negative reactions?

Structure of the relationship

In this section we will explore how the structure of worker-client relationships can undermine the very qualities it is meant to establish.

Social work literature usually attributes client dissatisfaction to clients' unrealistic expectations, inappropriate services, limited resources, or inadequate worker skills. Certainly some client dissatisfaction is due to such factors: sometimes it is impossible to know what services are most appropriate for a client; often particular services turn out to be unavailable. Sometimes workers lack the necessary knowledge, skill, or time for good service. And they may fail to convey empathy they genuinely feel or may convey racist or sexist attitudes of their own. Much has been written about these aspects of social service.

We must raise the question, however, of whether the problem lies deeper than the skill of workers or the availability of resources. We have only to look to comments from *satisfied* clients to see more clearly the ethical problems of the relationship and why many clients do not like "being helped."

> I really found out about Miss Coulson. When she's there she's not like a social worker. There's a lot of folk think you've got to watch what you say to them. . . . She was just the same as you, just a person with her own thoughts. A lot more people should go to these meetings.[19]

> He'll have a laugh and a joke, he's interested in you. . . . he's

> not one who rushes in, collects his pound and goes. He's interested in us as *people*, as a family.[20]

> It's got to be on a friendly basis with me. It's no good them coming and just sitting and listening to you, and not caring a damn, you know they don't. They don't *feel* for you. But when you get friends – say, for instance, you get a black eye – they really *feel* it with you. I got that impression with Pat – if she saw me with a black eye, you felt as if *she* felt it as well.[21]

Each of these clients contrasts the uninvolved, uncaring professional – identified as a social worker or official – with their own "friendly" worker. Client satisfaction and client change depended to some extent on client's perceptions of their workers as "friends."[22] And such friendship had the following qualities: empathy, caring, flexibility, patience, suggestions rather than advice, reciprocity in the form of sharing aspects of one's personal life, and immediate concrete help *in the mode requested.* In addition, many small social activities were viewed as important to befriending: "calling in for a cup of tea, accepting an invitation to a party, sending cards while on holiday, extending a home-visit to play with the children . . ."[23]

These clients did not seem to make a sharp distinction between "friend" and "professional" when they liked their worker. If a worker was only a professional and not a friend, the worker was usually viewed with hostility or at least distrust.

In addition to these qualities, clients cared about their workers' values. Sainsbury found that clients put a high priority on workers' moral goodness and "ethical integrity," although what this entailed was not entirely clear.[24] Sainsbury, along with Mayer and Timms, also found that clients were more apt to make positive changes in their lives if they identified with workers' values. And disclosures about the social worker's life were more acceptable when worker and client shared similar circumstances, hopes, and fantasies. If workers and clients differed sharply in values and background there was more chance of misunderstanding, less "befriending," and less change in social functioning. Studies of minority clients with white workers strengthen these findings.[25]

According to the studies, then, for casework to be effective workers must act like friends – conveying not only warmth, acceptance, caring, and empathy, but also some reciprocity in sharing, concrete help, social activities, common values and goals, and respect for the relationship as an end in itself. Social workers often try to provide some or all of these qualities but within carefully controlled limits. They monitor their interaction, because they have been taught that the purpose of the relationship is helping the client *through professional expertise.*[26] And here lies the crux of the conflict.

The goal of the professional relationship is to change the client, not to develop the relationship as a good in itself. Being a professional is different from being a friend. But as Sainsbury asks: "How far is personal concern for somebody compatible with the intention of changing him?"[27] If your chief goal is developing the relationship, then it seems you are not acting professionally to bring about specifiable change. If, however, your chief goal is to change the person, then ironically your personal concern will be manipulative. Your caring, therefore, is of an odd sort; it is not genuine in the sense of being for its own sake but created only in order to accomplish some other purpose.

> there is an increasing body of opinion that to make friendly relationships with people is justifiable in itself – it is its own good, and justifiable only in its own terms – and that to speak of a reason for forming a relationship is potentially unethical.[28]

If you form a relationship *for a reason*, then you are treating the relationship not as an end in itself but as a means to accomplishing your purpose. You thus run the risk of not fully respecting the person but exploiting the relationship in some way. On this argument, casework is inherently manipulative, with all the dangers of any manipulation, and the nature of the caring itself becomes suspect. Workers are caught in an impossible balancing act between genuine concern for their clients and manipulation of them. It is no wonder that clients do not know what to expect, nor that workers are sometimes unsure what constitutes appropriate caring.

Clients often do not fully understand the limited nature or

real purpose of the concern and empathy expressed by workers. While a "good" worker will try to convey these limitations to clients, the temptation is to minimize them in order to maximize the "friendly" aspects and thus ensure success in improving clients' lives. Once again, workers are caught in a balancing act, and clients do not know what to expect.

This tension in worker-client relationships can undermine the very objectives social workers seek – the respect, autonomy and empowerment of clients. Even if one argues that manipulation of clients is justified when it results in improved functioning, the danger is that such manipulation will be harmful. Workers are trained to think of clients in terms of diagnosing their problems and controlling the relationship in order to bring about specific results. As we have seen, this technique can easily lead to objectification of a client, condescension, and disregard of clients' perceptions, particularly if a client is passive or has different values from the worker. As one worker, a union leader, stated, "Most workers have spent a lot of years thinking their clients were either sick, incapable of taking care of themselves or deadbeats."[29] That is not easily balanced with genuine respect for a person.

In fact, it seems that the manipulative aspect of the relationship frequently wins out over the respectful one. We saw some of the results of such manipulative relationships in the earlier negative comments of both workers and clients. Such disrespect is not surprising, because the relationship is structured to be limited and thus partly manipulative. In addition, workers often cannot do the "caring" activities they want to do, because of their additional responsibilities to their agency or society, responsibilities which workers may not have adequately conveyed to clients.

Further, the notion of "learning the skills" of concern, empathy and genuineness has its own dangers. We can learn to act in ways that sometimes change our feelings. Assume, for example, that you want to learn to like your client, Alice, whom you strongly dislike. If you act as if you like her – greeting her warmly, listening to her carefully – you may begin to like her. You may search for some quality that you can like – her way of making coffee, for example – and try to build from that, or you may focus on how Alice's hard life has resulted in her unpleasant ways.

There are, however, no guarantees that our feelings will change in such situations, and there is a danger to the practice of pretending an acceptance or warmth we do not feel. We may mislead our clients as well as ourselves.

> The inestimable service that the psychotherapeutic ideology supplies is that it gives the individual the feeling that somebody cares – even if it is not true.[30]

While one might argue that such feigned feelings are sometimes beneficial to a client, it can also be argued that they create expectations which workers are not prepared to meet. Moreover, clients are not usually fooled by these gestures of concern and feel instead the full disrespect of such manipulation. "He gave you the impression that it was just his job, and he wasn't really interested." In addition, while such manipulation may be beneficial to a particular client, it may set up a destructive pattern of unreflectively thinking about all clients in manipulative terms.

"Authenticity" poses particular problems when considered *as a skill to be learned.* We must beware the dangers of a feigned, manipulative authenticity. Consider, for example, a textbook description of this skill:

> Authenticity is an interpersonal skill that *can be used* in all varieties of practice relationships, but it is particularly *useful* in collaborative relationships with clients. Authenticity involves disclosing oneself in particular ways and *involving oneself with a particular demeanor in a relationship.*[31] (my emphasis)

If a worker develops the appearance of authenticity in order to change a client, she is not really authentic. If feigned, the qualities of authenticity will not be genuine, not authentic. "An authentic person consciously holds little or nothing back in interactions with others," yet clearly the worker will be holding back the primary motivation for the "authenticity."[32]

As workers, we must consider how the structure of the

relationship – the limited "friendliness" and "authenticity" combined with the expert role – can all too easily result in undermining the autonomy and dignity of clients, rather than the reverse. Such undermining may result in the following ways:

(1) The client may not know what to expect and may be misled by a focus on "friendliness" to expect more than the worker can provide. Alternatively, the experienced client will know precisely how little to expect but may become embittered towards social workers.

(2) Because the worker as "expert" controls the interactions, she may not treat clients' perceptions and suggestions with the seriousness they deserve. That is, she may listen to a client's point of view, so that *she* can evaluate it and translate it back to the client, rather than being open to a real exchange of views. Ironically, then, the client's participation may be sharply limited by the worker's expertise. In viewing clients as less than equal participants, workers may end up treating them with subtle, and not so subtle, disrespect. The fact that client evaluations of service are rarely done is strong evidence of how little real seriousness is given to clients' perceptions.

(3) The lack of reciprocity built into the relationship may contribute to a client's sense of being unempowered. Because the relationship is supposed to be for the client's benefit and must be carefully controlled by the worker for this purpose, any reciprocity is limited. Clients, however, express uneasiness about the lack of reciprocity and about their seeming indebtedness.

> Sometimes it runs through my mind that they helped me out and I shouldn't ignore somebody that's helped me. Just because you've got over your troubles, you don't stop seeing somebody.[33]

> And then I started thinking: where am I going? What will they think of me? They'll think I'm a beggar. But I *had* to go, I *wanted* to go. And then, when I went, they gave me some beautiful clothes for the children. *Then* I was thinking: how can I repay? – taking with one hand, and not giving back with the other.[34]

These quotations remind us that few people like to feel indebted. To be the receiver of help, without being able to give back in kind, puts a person in an unequal position – a position of being dependent on others without their being dependent in return. Some workers recognize and make use of this position in a way that suggests the power of the "giver" and the possibilities for its misuse:

> Some of us do give with strings attached, in terms of some implicit bargain that if we do this for them they will do something for us, make some kind of effort.[35]

It is not surprising that clients want workers to share personal experiences, values or social activities to make the relationship more reciprocal. The relationship, however, is currently structured to have a limited reciprocity, and it may reinforce clients' sense of powerlessness and inequality, particularly when clients are already seriously unempowered relative to their workers.

To summarize, the worker-client relationship often undermines the very qualities it is meant to establish, and this irony is not simply the result of lack of skill or inadequate resources; instead, it appears to be inherent to the relationship itself. At the very least, the relationship has a strong potential for being undermined in the following ways:

(a) by the limited and thus partially manipulative empathy;
(b) by the nature of the professional role, with its conflicting responsibilities;
(c) by the lack of reciprocity in the relationship.

Workers should therefore carefully examine the kind of relationship they establish with each client:

> Am I acting ethically in the way I set up the relationship? Am I promoting the goals I believe in?
>
> Am I acting solely to establish an "effective" relationship but not necessarily an ethically desirable one?
>
> What sort of relationship is desirable?

The next section will examine the fundamental assumption of altruism in casework.

Professional altruism

In the nineteenth century, social workers thought of themselves as "friendly visitors" – they were friends to the poor but only within the bounds of their clear social, moral, and intellectual superiority. Their altruism was directed towards "the deserving" poor, who were expected to be grateful and were urged to take on their benefactors' moral outlook. Today, as social workers we are more apt to think of ourselves as experts, with special techniques that enable us to help others, regardless of their values. That expertise, however, still incorporates the notion of the "friendly" visitor – the trusted, caring helper – with all its original problems as well, but now more subtly hidden. As we saw in the previous section, the "friendly concern" of casework is often misleading and confusing to clients; it may undermine the very empowerment and respect it is intended to create.

In this section, we will examine some of the fundamental assumptions which lie at the heart of social work and which contribute to the problematic casework relationship – assumptions about altruism and benevolence.

Like our nineteenth-century counterparts, we tend to assume that altruism is desirable and helpful; by definition it is concern for the good of others. Benevolence also, the inclination to do good, seems unquestionably desirable. We assume further that professional altruism and benevolence, helping on the basis of our expertise, empowers clients. Social work is based on these assumptions.

Unlike our nineteenth-century predecessors, however, we are aware of the harm that can be done in the name of altruism. Much has been written about the ill-effects of good intentions.

> Virtually every caring system we have keeps its eye on the good it hopes to accomplish and blinks at the harm it is doing. As a result, hundreds of thousands – perhaps millions – of people are violated every day of their lives by the encroachments of their ostensible benefactors.[36]

In the name of the "best interests" of clients and of "expert knowledge" of those interests, social workers and other helping professionals have sometimes harmed clients and have often violated their rights.

> Family court judges argued that it was necessary to "search" a welfare mother's house without a warrant in order to find out if her child was being abused. The New York State Department of Social Services supported solitary confinement in children's institutions as necessary to the overall rehabilitative purposes of confinement. Housing officials defended evictions of entire families by claiming that such evictions were necessary to protect other residents. Psychiatrists in Florida justified the fifteen-year incarceration, without treatment, of a nondangerous "patient" in a mental "hospital" by claiming, in effect, that incarceration itself was therapeutic.[37]

The misuse of benevolence, however, has not led to a general questioning of its desirability. Instead, critics seek to limit the harm of good intentions and good works through focus on justice and human rights.

> It is not benevolence we should abandon, but rather the naive faith that benevolence can mitigate the mischievousness of power so feared by those who wrote our Bill of Rights. . . . Just as the liberty interests of the governed cannot be the concern of their governors, so the liberty interests of the needy cannot be the concern of their benefactors. They both mean to govern well, *but they mean to govern.* They therefore must be "bitted and bridled by a Bill of Rights."[38]

We must evaluate, then, at least two perspectives on benevolence in social work – benevolence as a gift and client rights which define and limit benevolence.

If clients have a right to services of various sorts, then they have a moral claim to those services, whereas if there is no such right, they are dependent on the good will of others. "While gratitude is never the appropriate response to receiving one's due, it is always the appropriate response to receiving gratuitous aid."[39] The right to a certain level of well-being, then, makes clients the equal of others in society and promotes a corresponding respect. Without such a right, clients are dependent on the good will of others, and the stigma of dependence promotes a subordinate status and lack of respect.

The debate about whether welfare should be viewed as a right or a gift is a complex one that cannot be settled here. In doing casework, however, we make assumptions about altruism and client rights and we must clarify these assumptions in order to understand fully the ethical positions we are taking.

Social work, with its emphasis on expert help, presupposes that doing for others is good. According to one position, if society is constructed to promote altruism (through voluntary contributions, volunteer work, and private social services), then the society will also promote a sense of community and enriched relationships, with a sense of responsibility to others. Titmuss makes such a case in *The Gift Relationship*.[40]

This perspective, however, is primarily from the point of view of the *giver* or *doer* of good and does not adequately account for the potential misuses and arbitrariness of such altruism, nor for the uneasiness its benefactors feel. As we saw in the last section, the inherent inequality of altruism makes its goodness suspect. (1) If *we*, rather than *clients*, determine what is needed or good, then clients are often made to feel more dependent and more powerless by the process. (2) Respect is undermined by the inequality altruism fosters: we simply find it harder to respect people whom we view as dependent on us and unequal to us in competence and judgment. (3) Clients feel unequal if they are always the recipients of altruism and never the givers of it. They express their uneasiness through their desire to "repay" a worker in some way, so as to make the relationship an equal and respectful one. "*Then* I was thinking: how can I repay? – taking with one hand, and not giving back with the other."[41]

No one likes a relationship in which she or he is always the recipient of generosity. Altruism is desirable between equals, when the possibility of reciprocity is assumed. As Chavez stated, a nurturing society "will be one where the ideal of altruism will have no meaning, because everyone will acknowledge mutual needs."[42]

Altruism, then, suffers from its inherent inequality, its focus on *doing for* another person, and this "doing for" is basic to casework. We need to question our one-sided altruism and models of empowerment based upon it.

These problems in the casework relationship are not solved simply by adding clients' rights, as is sometimes supposed. There are at least two serious problems with adding a rights perspective to casework.

(1) To be an advocate for clients' rights, you must first decide what rights a client has – a right to welfare benefits, health care, day-care, job training, education, or what? There are radical disagreements about this within society. Workers disagree among themselves, as do workers with their clients. You will be an advocate for particular rights. If your client disagrees with your view then, in addition, you must decide whether to respect the client's view or to act on your "expert" opinion of clients' rights, in opposition to your client.

(2) Concepts such as "clients' rights" or "the right to welfare" cover a wide variety of different services and actions; they thus also cover over conflicting views about rights and welfare. In particular, they obscure the quite different roles which are part of being a "client advocate." If we accept and promote client rights, we must still balance the role of expert judge of client "needs" with the role of advocate of client rights, and the two roles are often incompatible.

We cannot resolve these sorts of conflicts by diligently focusing on casework as if it were apolitical, nor by abstractly comparing different social welfare perspectives. We must confront the dismaying array of conflicts *in our actual practice* and decide what sort of worker-client relationship to establish. Doing so will require taking a position about the desirability of altruism, the nature of clients' rights and the sort of empowerment one wishes to foster. Not all the conflicts are resolvable, but in understanding them and being clear about our fundamental assumptions, we can avoid undermining the autonomy of clients and may be able to develop new ways of thinking about "helping others."

We must consider one additional conflict. Altruism in casework is professional altruism, that is, helping on the basis of expertise but also helping for a salary. Altruism is part of our job, and this alters its nature significantly. It establishes an inherent conflict between doing what we think is best for the client and doing what will preserve or enhance our work status. Although this conflict is reflected in the Code of Ethics' statement of social workers' responsibilities both to client and her agency, the Code says little to resolve the conflict. In Chapter 6, on bureaucracy, we saw that these responsibilities often conflict and thus limit what a social worker can or is willing to do for a client.

> I've been in the children's network for four years, always working myself ragged doing what I could to advocate, coordinate, or somehow make the system work for children. I've been praised by supervisors for my energy, but I still have no security, a low salary, and a sense that the kids I work with are never going to get real help. My friends who can are going to graduate schools or moving. I've got a family and I guess I'm looking for one of those cushy bureaucratic jobs I've always criticized. What else can I do?[43]

Many professional social workers, like this youth worker, care deeply about the welfare of their clients and work overtime under difficult conditions. They also have their own welfare to consider. Their "caring concern" will usually be constrained by their concern for their own careers. And as we have seen, clients may suffer from the ambiguities inherent in receiving help from the "caring" expert who is trying to balance so many different obligations.

If we accept this analysis of professional altruism and its inherent problems, what does this mean for the practice of social work? Does it mean abandoning social work altogether? Will we not then simply make society even less humane than it already is?

Given the inequities and poverty that exist in our society, abandoning professional altruism altogether would result in greater harm than good. Such abandonment would result in even greater inequality and injustice than we now have, because it would not necessarily be replaced by anything more adequate.

The questioning of altruism – of doing for others – should lead, however, to rethinking and possibly restructuring the worker-client relationship to avoid the worst aspects of altruism and to make us sensitive to its possible abuses. Perhaps we can begin to construct new ways of empowering others.

Recommendations

Let us return to the cases of Maria and of Alice (pages 158–60). Suppose that after a few months of treatment Maria wants to be friends and asks you to have lunch on a regular basis. Suppose that Alice begins to confide her infractions of welfare rules. What sort of relationship can you establish that is honest, respectful and empowering to the client?

A particular action of the client or worker may abruptly bring to the surface the different expectations of each. When Maria requests that you regularly have lunch, she reveals her expectation of friendship which conflicts with your assumption of how a "professional" behaves. Even if you are clear about the nature and limits of the relationship at the beginning, Maria may misinterpret or forget what you say. Studies of clients' and workers' perceptions reveal a great deal of this sort of misunderstanding. As the following passage, introduced in Chapter 3, summarizes:

> There is almost a Kafkaesque quality about these worker-client interactions. To exaggerate only slightly, each of the parties assumed that the other shared certain of his underlying conceptions about behavior and the ways in which it might be altered. Then, unaware of the inappropriateness of his extrapolations, each found special reasons to account for the other's conduct.[44]

While clarity about goals and expectations is essential from the start, it will not settle the central question: what sort of relationship should you establish? What will be respectful and empowering to the client? There are no general answers to these questions, because clients' situations differ radically, as do workers' resources, training, and available time. Each case has to be considered separately, but a worker's decisions will reflect her underlying assumptions.

After your first few appointments with Maria, for example, you may decide that casework is not desirable. Because of its inherent inequality, you believe it will accentuate the already great differences between the two of you. You may also believe that the "caring" will be manipulative and misleading. You may limit your role to suggesting group activities for Maria, as well as informing her of needed adjunct services, such as food stamps or English language classes.

You may, on the other hand, believe that casework would greatly benefit Maria, perhaps because of the severity of her depression. In this case, you may also decide to encourage acts of reciprocity, so as not to increase her sense of powerlessness and indebtedness. You may determine the limits of the relationship through mutual negotiation. This would include discussion of your conflicting obligations, of the social and political goals on which you base your help, and so on.

The nature of your casework with Maria will depend on your ethical and political position: you may act as the "neutral, objective" insight therapist or you may try to enlist Maria as a potential "comrade" in the struggle to achieve common social work goals; these differences were discussed in Chapter 4. They affect the content of the therapy and the nature of the relationship.

In the case of Alice, who is on welfare and in need of additional services, you should be clear at the start about what she can expect. If you attempt to be the caring, trusted helper, you should clarify the limits of that help. You should consider whether your goal is to empower Alice, and if so, how far you are willing to fight your agency or risk your job in order to achieve your goal. If you believe you can or should do little to help Alice, you should not mislead her into thinking that you can do more.

In some situations, help in the form of psychiatric casework may serve to empower clients. This is most apt to be true when clients fully understand and accept the assumptions of casework, when their outlook and backgrounds are similar to the therapist's, and when they have real choice. Social workers' private therapy practices might be one example. In other situations, for example seriously disturbed clients who come regularly to a mental health clinic, psychiatric casework may not be desirable. We must be cautious about using an inherently unequal relationship to establish equality.

The following suggestions may help us to begin thinking

about ways to restructure the relationship, drawing on the discussions in previous chapters.

(1) We need to find ways to create reciprocity, if we want to empower clients. Increasingly, social workers have recognized the importance and effectiveness of self-help and advocacy groups, where genuine reciprocity and friendship can flourish. These groups, however, are usually viewed as adjuncts to professional help, which remains unchanged. We must consider changing professional help itself to make the relationship more mutual. Clients should be asked to evaluate the services they receive. They should participate in larger numbers on the boards of social service agencies. If client-representatives at least sometimes attended staff meetings, the rights of clients might be more carefully protected and clients addressed more respectfully. These actions can be quite threatening, since they may lead clients to challenge their workers. They make clear, however, that we do not always recommend to our clients what would empower them, even though that is one of our espoused goals.

(2) In addition, workers should consider ways in which clients will feel less indebted. Here our underlying political assumptions emerge as a powerful determinant of the relationship. While many social workers believe that society owes clients services because of inequities in the society, on some other level they believe that clients only "deserve" services if they meet certain conditions – that they find a job, try harder, stop having children, etc. Workers should probe their own political beliefs, so as to understand the perceptions that inform their approach to the relationship.

(3) As workers, we should be more explicit with clients, not only about the goals of treatment, but about our own beliefs regarding social service, fundamental values, and the limits of the relationship. Only in this way can clients know what to expect and thereby avoid feeling confused, bewildered, or angry. Such disclosure is particularly important because of the worker's conflicting responsibilities to client, agency, colleagues, profession, and society. A worker will not be able to specify a precise ranking of responsibilities, but can give clients a sense of the limits of client advocacy and give them the opportunity to challenge the worker directly.

This process would also serve to make us more aware of our

own beliefs. In explaining our assumptions to clients, we may then begin to reconsider, justify, and so possibly reformulate our beliefs.

(4) Workers should consider forming groups among themselves to protest actions by the agency. As we have seen, bureaucratic structure tends to undermine workers' sense of moral responsibility and to cause them to feel responsible to the agency rather than the client. If workers are to help clients, they must build alliances that will enable them to speak out and to say no.

> I've learned that the world doesn't stop if you say "no." Now when they want me to do the impossible I say "no, it's impossible, we have to do some other thing instead" – I always have an option ready. At first people were shocked but I've found that I usually win because they know I won't give in and that my suggestions usually work because I know the community.[45]

(5) Another recommendation is that we find ways to make clients aware of our political agendas. Social work's mission has always gone beyond changing the client to changing the society which undermines client-functioning. Today, workers often separate that larger context of social reform from their relationships to clients. A worker does *individual* casework with clients and then in addition lobbies the legislature for reform in mental health. We justify this separation by saying that clients are not interested in "being political" and that we should not impose our social reform agendas on them. Some clients are indeed uninterested or incapable of such involvement. Since, however, the worker helps clients in a social context, she necessarily makes assumptions of what that context should be. By not sharing her political agenda in some way with clients, a worker deprives them of knowing her perspective and thus also deprives each of them of an opportunity to act as more of an equal, either with or against the worker.

Whatever options we consider, we must constantly reflect on the impact we have on clients: are we creating an atmosphere of mutual respect? Are we empowering clients or merely ourselves? And what do our clients have to say about the services we provide?

8 Realizing our purpose

In each chapter, we have seen how *ethical conflict* is inherent to human service practice: conflict in our responsibilities to clients, agency, profession, society and in our ethical and political points of view. This book argues for a *process of thinking about* these conflicts, rather than for a specific ethical or political program.

To realize our purpose, even to understand what it is, we must engage in dialogue with each other and be willing to take seriously points of view different from our own. Through this process, we can begin to recognize the complex ethical and political conflicts embedded in our work and to acknowledge inconsistencies between our goals and our practice. We can begin to develop a coherent practice, grounded in ethical and political assumptions that we understand and can justify.

In conclusion, then, I shall suggest some ways in which we can begin to create an atmosphere of ethical questioning and debate within social work practice.

First, I present an outline for an ethical analysis of agencies – a way to begin examination of ethical issues we face in our workplace. Second, I suggest questions which can help us analyze the kinds of relationships we have to clients and therefore the sort of empowerment or autonomy we encourage. Finally, I shall consider briefly the role of ethical experts and of a code of ethics in helping or hampering us to realize our purpose.

Ethical analysis of an agency

Pretend that you have been hired as a consultant to do an ethical analysis of your agency. You are to submit a report of serious and pervasive ethical issues confronted in your workplace and to make recommendations for tackling them.

This exercise can be useful in several ways. It forces you to step back from daily tasks to examine the overall context of your work – what does the agency do? What should it do? What population does it and should it serve? How does your work fit into the general functioning of the agency?

Outlining these ethical issues can result in a clearer understanding of your own point of view. The outline will consist of issues *you* consider important. Do others in the agency disagree with you? On what grounds? What about your clients? What priorities do you give to the issues you list? What reasons can you give for considering one issue more important or serious than another?

If you work for a large agency, this task may seem overwhelming and analyzing a smaller unit within the agency may be more useful.

The following outline can help you begin the process of identifying ethical issues. The questions are not exhaustive but intended to begin a process of thinking about the issues.

Ethical issues in an agency

(1) Moral issues presented by the goals and overall functioning of the agency –
stated goals versus actual goals;
agency goals versus your own goals;
agency demands versus professional demands.

(2) Moral issues presented by employer-employee relations –
union issues – unionizing, strikes, harassment of union,
bureaucratic issues – incompetent supervisors or co-workers, unethical rules, favoritism, etc.;
issues of confidentiality;
racial, sexual or class issues.

(3) Moral issues presented by worker-client relationships –
union issues – worker vs. client demands;
confidentiality;
coercion – informed consent;
racial, sexual or class issues;
morality of therapeutic techniques.

(4) Moral issues presented by agency's relations to other agencies.

(5) Moral issues presented by agency-community relations.
(6) Other union issues.
(7) Other important issues.

Understanding your own assumptions

Our ethical point of view begins with our earliest experiences. By the time we are adults, we have quite sophisticated justifications for the ways we behave, and these may or may not coincide with our actual behavior. We can sometimes learn more about our personal point of view by looking at its history. While the following questions may seem impossibly broad, they can give us insight into what we believe:

(1) What goals are most important *to you* in your human service work?
(2) How did you come to hold these goals? What in your experience has led you to the goals you now hold?

There is another, even more important set of questions to ask. If we focus exclusively on the client and speak, as we often do, solely in terms of vague goals like empowerment we may escape from understanding our ethical positions. We need questions that force us to examine what we gain from the work we do.

Consider the following questions:

(1) Do you need your clients?
(2) What do you want or need from them?
(3) What do you gain from them?

We sometimes forget that the relationship is two-way. We want something from our clients, in order to enjoy our work. We do not often enough stop to examine what we are getting. If our services were no longer needed, how would we feel? Do we need our clients in order to feel worthwhile, feel normal, do research, have job security, have social status, grow intellectually, or what?

We are indebted to our clients in lots of ways which we do not usually acknowledge or examine. They are apt to be the basis of articles we write, our clinical reputation, our sense of leading a worthwhile life or being an interesting person. Through examining these questions, we can gain a clearer understanding of the values we hold and the ways we may "hold onto" or "dis-able" clients in order to serve *our needs*.

We would be better served if we changed the model of *expert* social worker and *deficient* client. We too are needy, and served by finding clients who can meet our needs. If we begin to look at our work in this way, we may gain a better understanding of our vested interests in being "professional." And we may move closer to giving our clients the respect and autonomy we say is the basis of our work.

Ethical experts

I cannot be completely opposed to ethical experts and consistently be the author of this book. Still, the role of ethical expert is a dangerous one which has only a limited usefulness. Ethical experts can help to shake us up or to point out problems. As stated in Chapter 6, however, the danger is that ethical issues will be designated as the expert's province rather than the concern of everyone in an agency. An "expert" in ethics should never be in the position of giving "the right answer." That should only emerge from discussion among all those involved. In addition, an ethical expert, because he or she is usually not engaged in the "front-line" work of the agency, will be in some respects an outsider and thus may have little credibility. The expert may serve the function of making the agency look good ("we have an ethical expert!") while in effect being discounted within the agency itself.

Code of Ethics

Of social workers I have asked, perhaps two or three have ever read the existing N.A.S.W. Code of Ethics. But even if the Code were read more widely, social workers would not be much helped in resolving ethical issues, for the Code simply restates the conflicting responsibilities discussed throughout this book. Further, as I have argued, no one code should guide social work practice, because there are several conflicting points of view which merit consideration. Any existing code will be misleading if it tries to define a unified set of values.

The Code of Ethics has been revised several times, but by a

relatively small group within the profession. At this point, what is needed is much broader debate about the ethical and political basis of our work. Given the different points of view that exist in the profession, the Code could serve as a focal point for such dialogue. This should take place, however, without the expectation that we necessarily will or should arrive at a professional consensus about the sort of society we are trying to create. What we need to stress instead are the values of disagreement and of questioning.

Although dialogue can degenerate into a mean-spirited, hostile exchange, in which one displays superiority or becomes entrenched in a narrow-minded view, it need not do so. Such exchanges would in fact be better termed monologues, or diatribes, than dialogue. Real dialogue assumes a willingness to listen and an openness to new possibilities. Through dialogue, we become more aware of the positions we hold; in defending them, we learn their limitations. Together we can question, disagree, construct alternatives. It is to such dialogue that I hope this book will contribute.

Notes

1 Facing dilemmas

1 Cicero, quoted in Montaigne, *Complete Essays of Montaigne*, trans. by Donald M. Frame, Stanford, Stanford University Press, 1958, p. 133.

2 Many social work writers talk about the importance of serving the most needy. See, for example, W. Richan and A. R. Mendelsohn, *Social Work. The Unloved Profession*, N.Y., New Viewpoints, 1973; or B. Reynolds, *An Uncharted Journey, Fifty Years of Growth in Social Work*, N.Y., Citadel, 1963.

3 Of 4.3 million "service professionals" 3 million are in the public sector. See A. Withorn, *Serving the People. Social Services and Social Change*, N.Y., Columbia University, 1984, p. 159. Her statistics are taken from D. Johnson and C. O'Donnell, "The Accumulation Crisis and Service Professionals," in K. Fox *et al.*, *Crisis in the Public Sector. A Reader*, N.Y., Monthly Review Press, 1982, p. 34.

4 Standard texts on social work practice make some reference to ethical issues but do not examine the ethical issues in any depth. See, for example, C. D. Garvin and B. A. Seabury, *Interpersonal Practice in Social Work*, N. J., Prentice-Hall, 1984; A. Kadushin, *Social Work Interview*, second edn, N.Y., Columbia, 1983. There are many other examples.

5 See, for example, I. Illich, "Disabling Professions," in I. Illich, I. Zola, J. McKnight, J. Caplan and H. Shaiken, *Disabling Professions*, London, Marion Boyars, 1977; or W. Gaylin, I. Glasser, S. Marcus and D. Rothman, *Doing Good. The Limits of Benevolence*, N.Y., Pantheon, 1978.

6 This issue is discussed at the level of social policy but is not always sufficiently recognized at the level of case decisions.

7 See, for example, David Cooper, *The Death of the Family*, N.Y., Pantheon, 1970; S. Firestone, *The Dialectic of Sex*, N.Y., Bantam, 1971; Carol B. Stack, *All Our Kin*, N.Y., Harper & Row, 1974; H. Cohen, *Equal Rights for Children*, Totowa, N. J., Rowman & Littlefield, 1980.

8 See, for example, Salvador Minuchin *et al.*, *Families and Family Therapy*, Cambridge, Mass., Harvard University Press, 1974; C. Madanes, *Strategic Family Therapy*, San Francisco, Jossey-Bass, 1981. For exceptions to this approach, see, for example, M. Greenspan, *A New Approach to Women and Therapy*, N.Y.,

McGraw-Hill, 1983; and R. H. Dana (ed.), *Human Services for Cultural Minorities*, Baltimore University Park Press, 1981.

9 I do not know of any statistics to support this claim. I am relying on my own experience and that of social workers I have interviewed, as well as the analyses in textbooks on social work practice.

10 See N. Timms, *Social Work Values: An Enquiry*, London, Routledge & Kegan Paul, 1983, Chs 1 and 2; C. Levy, "On the Development of a Code of Ethics," *Social Work*, 19 (March 1974), pp. 207–16; F. M. Lowenberg, "Professional Values and Professional Ethics in Social Work Education," in B. Baer and R. Federico, *Educating the Baccalaurate Social Worker*, Cambridge, Ballinger, 1978.

11 *Code of Ethics of the National Association of Social Workers*, Washington, D.C., N.A.S.W. 1980.

12 *National Republican Party Platform*, Washington, D.C., Republican National Committee, 1984.

13 C. S. Levy, *Social Work Ethics*, N.Y., Human Sciences, 1976; F. G. Reamer, *Ethical Dilemmas in Social Service*, N.Y., Columbia, 1982.

14 C. S. Levy, *op. cit.*, pp. 105, 106.

15 *Ibid.*, p. 112, from A. Edel, "Anthropology and Ethics in Common Focus," *Journal of Royal Anthropology Institute*, 92 (Part 1), 1962, p. 70.

16 Abraham Edel, "Science and the Structure of Ethics," *International Encyclopedia of Unified Science*, Vol. 2, No. 3, Chicago, University of Chicago Press, 1961, particularly Part 2.

17 A. Gewirth, *Reason and Morality*, Chicago, University of Chicago Press, 1978.

18 J. Rawls, *A Theory of Justice*, Cambridge, Mass., Harvard University, 1971; R. Nozick, *Anarchy, State and Utopia*, N.Y., Basic Books, 1974; A. MacIntyre, *After Virtue. A Study in Moral Theory*, Indiana, Notre Dame Press, 1981.

19 Radical social work accounts differ among themselves. I am drawing on the accounts of J. Galper, *Social Work Practice. A Radical Perspective*, N.J., Prentice-Hall, 1980 and J. Galper, *The Politics of Social Services*, N.J., Prentice-Hall, 1975; R. Bailey and M. Brake (eds), *Radical Social Work*, N.Y., Pantheon, 1976; D. Stratham, *Radicals in Social Work*, London, Routledge & Kegan Paul, 1978; P. Corrigan and P. Leonard, *Social Work Practice Under Capitalism, A Marxist Approach*, London, Macmillan, 1978; A. Withorn, *op. cit.*

20 See I. Illich, *op. cit.*

21 For one example of an alternative Code of Ethics, see J. Galper, *The Politics of Social Services*, N.J., Prentice-Hall, 1975, pp. 224–7.

22 One exception to this is F. Loewenberg and R. Dolgoff, *Ethical Decisions for Social Work Practice*, Itasca, Ill., Peacock, 1972; the

analyses of cases are very limited and are not tied to different underlying ethical bases. N. Timms's *Social Work Values: An Enquiry*, *op. cit.*, is an excellent introduction to ethical issues and makes some points similar to mine. It does not, however, use the case method.

2 Unraveling ethical assumptions

1 William Blake, *Jerusalem*, sec. 55.

2 There has been much recent discussion about the domain of ethics and its relation to the good life. See, for example, B. Williams, *Ethics and the Limits of Philosophy*, Cambridge, Mass., Harvard University, 1985.

3 See J. S. Mill, *On Liberty*, ed. by E. Rapaport, Indianapolis, Hackett, 1978, and *Utilitarianism, with Critical Essays*, ed. by S. Gorovitz, Indianapolis, Bobbs-Merrill, 1971. See also J. Bentham, *The Utilitarians: An Introduction to the Principles of Morals and Legislation*, N.Y., Doubleday, 1961. For a good introductory discussion of utilitarianism, see J. C. Smart and B. Williams, *Utilitarianism: For and Against*, Cambridge, Cambridge University, 1973.

4 See I. Kant, *Foundations of the Metaphysics of Morals, and What is Enlightenment?*, trans. by L. W. Beck, N.Y., Liberal Arts, 1959.

5 *Ibid.*, p. 40.

6 *Ibid.*

7 There are many different rights-based theories. For a good introductory discussion, see J. Feinberg, *Rights, Justice and the Bounds of Liberty: Essays in Social Philosophy*, Princeton, Princeton University, 1980 or *Social Philosophy*, Englewood Cliffs, N.J., Prentice-Hall, 1973; for two influential, contemporary rights-based theories, see J. Rawls, *A Theory of Justice*, Cambridge, Mass., Belknap, 1971 and R. Nozick, *Anarchy, State and Utopia*, N.Y., Basic Books, 1974.

8 See, for example, M. Friedman, *Capitalism and Freedom*, Chicago, Phoenix, 1963; see also, George Gilder, *Wealth and Poverty*, N.Y., Basic Books, 1981.

9 See, for example, Carl Wellman, *Welfare Rights*, Totowa, N.J., Rowman & Littlefield, 1981.

10 F. Reamer, *Ethical Dilemmas in Social Service*, N.Y., Columbia, 1982.

11 See also Gewirth, *Reason and Morality*, Chicago, University of Chicago Press, 1978.

12 Reamer, *op. cit.*, p. 72, from Gewirth, *op. cit.*, p. 135.

13 Reamer, *op. cit.*, p. 71.

14 There are many Marxist theories, with significant differences among them, and many disagreements even about the tenets of Marx's theory. The account I give is based on writings of Marx; see, for example, K. Marx, *Early Writings*, trans. by T. B. Bottomore, N.Y., McGraw-Hill, 1964 and K. Marx, *Capital: A*

Critique of Political Economy, ed. by F. Engels, N.Y., International Publishers, 1967. For one recent, clear exposition of the Marxist position, see A. Jagger, *Feminist Politics and Human Nature*, N.J., Rowman & Allenheld, 1983.

15 For one such position, see W. D. Ross, *The Right and the Good*, Oxford, Clarendon Press, 1930.

16 Again, there are many different virtue-based theories. My comments draw particularly on the following accounts: Plato, *The Collected Dialogues of Plato*, ed by E. Hamilton, N.Y., Pantheon, 1964; Aristotle, "The Nicomachean Ethics," in *The Basic Works of Aristotle*, ed by R. McKeon, N.Y., Random House, 1941; *The Philokalia. The Complete Text*, compiled by St Nikodimos of the Holy Mountain and St Makarios of Corinth, trans. by Palmer, *et al.*, Vol. I, London, Faber & Faber, 1979; I. Murdoch, *The Sovereignty of Good*, N.Y., Schocken, 1971; and A. MacIntyre, *After Virtue. A Study in Moral Theory*, Indiana, Notre Dame Press, 1981.

17 *Ibid.*

18 See, for example, J. Heschel (ed.), *Between God and Man. An Interpretation from the Writings of Abraham J. Heschel*, N.Y., Free Press, 1959.

19 See W. May, "The Virtues in a Professional Setting," *Soundings, An Interdisciplinary Journal*, Vol. 67, No. 3 (Fall, 1984), pp. 245–66.

20 This idea is developed in Chapter 7.

21 For a useful introductory discussion of relativism, see B. Williams, *Morality: An Introduction to Ethics*, N.Y., Harper & Row, 1972.

22 This account still requires an explanation of what counts as "rational evaluation" and of whether rationality itself is relative. The issue is a complex one, which cannot be addressed here. For some interesting discussion, see, for example, Bryan R. Wilson (ed.), *Rationality*, N.Y., Harper & Row, 1970.

3 Violating confidentiality

1 Tarasoff v. Regents of the University of California, 118 Calif. Rep. 129, 529 p 2nd 553, 1974.

2 "Privacy v. Fair Trail. A Rhode Island Rape-Crisis Center forces the issue of confidentiality," by R. Vaughan and M. Matza, *Boston Pheonix*, Section 1, 8 March 1983, p. 10.

3 *Code of Professional Responsibility and Code of Judicial Conduct*, Chicago, American Bar Assoc., 1976.

4 The restrictions on doctors and psychiatrists are regulated primarily by state law. Some states have granted the psychiatrist-patient relationship practically absolute protection. See J. Dubey, "Confidentiality as a Requirement of the Therapist: Technical Necessities for Absolute Privilege in psychotherapy," *American Journal of Psychiatry*, 131, pp. 1093–6, 1974.

5 For a good, short discussion of these differences among professions, see S. Wilson, *Confidentiality in Social Work, Issues and Principles*, London, Free Press, 1978.
6 *Ibid.*
7 *Ibid.*
8 Not all such cases have to be reported to the District Attorney. For a fuller description, see Chapter 288 of Acts and Resolves of Commonwealth of Massachusetts, 1983.
9 Francis Koestler (ed.), *The COMSTAC Report: Standards for Strengthened Services*, N.Y., Commission on Standards and Accreditation of Services for the Blind, 1966, p. 33; M. Reynolds, "Threats to Confidentiality," *Social Work Journal*, Vol. 21, No. 2 (March 1976), p. 109. Both of these are taken from Wilson, *op. cit.*, pp. 1 and 2.
10 See Wilson, *op. cit.*, for illustrations of this.
11 This information is based on interviews with doctors as well as social workers.
12 This was the solution adopted by the Rhode Island Rape-Crisis Center, whose case of confidentiality was quoted at the beginning of the chapter.
13 The issue of whether there are unconscious motivations and of what the criteria would be for establishing them lies beyond the scope of this book. I wish simply to draw attention to the ways in which the concept of unconscious motivation can be used to obscure other issues. Many others have also written about this. See, for example, R. D. Laing, *The Divided Self. A Study of Sanity and Madness*, Chicago, Quadrangle Books, 1960, or A. MacIntyre, *The Unconscious. A Conceptual Analysis*, London, Routledge & Kegan Paul, 1958.
14 S. Bok, *Secrets. On the Ethics of Concealment and Revelation*, N.Y., Pantheon, 1982, Ch. IX.
15 *Ibid.*, p. 120.
16 See H. L. Ruben and D. D. Ruben, "Confidentiality and Privileged Communication: The Psychotherapeutic Relationship Revisited," *Medical Annals of the District of Columbia*, 41 (1972); L. Roth and A. Meisel, "Dangerousness, Confidentiality and the Duty to Warn," *American Journal of Psychiatry*, 134, 1977, pp. 508–11; H. Gurevitz, "*Tarasoff*: Protective Privilege versus Public Peril," *American Journal of Psychiatry*, 134, 1977, pp. 289–92.
17 See, for example, H. H. Perlman, *Relationship, The Heart of Helping People*, Chicago, University of Chicago, 1979.
18 S. Wilson raises similar points in her book on confidentiality. She argues that we do not yet know what limits confidentiality should have. We need to know more about clients' expectations of confidentiality, its importance in maintaining relationships, and the harm it may do. See Wilson, *op.cit.*
19 Bok, *op. cit.*, p. 103.
20 See Chapter 2 for a fuller description of Kantian and utilitarian ethical views.

21 For others making this same point, see, for example, A. MacIntyre, *A Short History of Ethics*, N.Y., Macmillan, 1966, Prentice-Hall, 1973.
22 See B. Williams, "A Critique of Utilitarianism," in J. Smart and B. Williams, *Utilitarianism: For and Against*, Cambridge, Cambridge University Press, 1973.
23 Bok, *op. cit.*, pp. 15–18.
24 These inequalities are apparent in E. Mayer and N. Timms, *The Client Speaks. Working Class Impressions of Casework*, N.Y., Atherton, 1970.
25 See *Ibid*, Ch. 1, for a review of some of this literature. See also, R. Pomeroy, H. Yahr and L. Podell, *Reactions of Welfare Clients to Caseworker Contact*, N.Y., City University, 1969; S. Rees, *Social Work Face to Face*, N.Y., Columbia, 1979; E. Sainsbury, *Social Work with Families. Perceptions of Social Casework among Clients of a Family Service Unit*, London, Routledge & Kegan Paul, 1975.
26 Mayer and Timms, *op.cit.*, p. 155.
27 *Ibid.*, pp. 155–8.
28 See, for example, R. Dana (ed), *Human Services for Cultural Minorities*, Baltimore, University Park Press, 1981.
29 Mayer and Timms, *op. cit.*, Ch. 10.
30 *Ibid.*, p. 187.
31 *Ibid.*, p. 127.
32 *Ibid.*, Appendix 3.
33 *Ibid.*, p. 77.
34 See note 16.
35 "Neo-Freudian" covers a wide assortment of theories. I am referring to object-relations theory, which has particularly influenced psychiatric casework. For a good introduction to this therapeutic approach, see H. Guntrip, *Psychoanalytic Theory, Therapy, and the Self. A Basic Guide to the Human Personality in Freud, Erikson, Klein, Sullivan, Fairbairn, Hartmann, Jacobson and Winnicott*, N.Y., Basic Books, 1971.
36 H. T. Engelhardt, Jr, "Psychotherapy as Meta-ethics," *Psychiatry*, 36 (1973), pp. 440–5; see in particular p. 442.
37 See, for example, P. R. Breggin, "Psychiatry and Psychotherapy as Political Processes," *American Journal of Psychotherapy* (July 1975), Vol. 29, No. 3.
38 A great deal has been written on this. For one standard text see C. Brenner, *An Elementary Textbook of Psychoanalysis*, N.Y., International Universities Press, 1975.
39 See T. B. Karasu, "The Ethics of Psychotherapy," in R. B. Edwards (ed.), *Psychiatry and Ethics, Insanity, Rational Autonomy and Mental Health Care*, Buffalo, N.Y., Prometheus, 1982, particularly pp. 154, 155.
40 See, for example, J. Galper, *The Politics of Social Services*, N.J., Prentice-Hall, 1975; and A. Withorn, *Serving the People. Social Services and Social Change*, N.Y., Columbia University, 1984.

4 Influencing the client: whose values are promoted?

1 Paul Halmos, *The Faith of the Counsellors, A Study in the Theory and Practice of Social Casework and Psychotherapy*, N.Y., Schocken, 1966, p. 177.

2 G. Bermant, H. Kelman and D. Warwick (eds), *The Ethics of Social Intervention*, N.Y., John Wiley, 1978, p. 385.

3 For the central importance of counseling in casework, see, for example, H. H. Perlman, *Relationship, The Heart of Helping People*, Chicago, University of Chicago, 1979; or Paul Halmos, *op. cit.*

4 S. L. Halleck, *The Politics of Therapy*, N.Y., Science House, 1971, p. 19.

5 Engelhardt takes this position: H. T. Engelhardt, Jr, "Psychotherapy as Meta-Ethics," *Psychiatry*, 36 (Nov. 1973), pp. 440–5. See also, for example, E. Erickson, *Childhood and Society*, N.Y., Norton, 1950; or A. H. Maslow, *Toward a Psychology of Being*, N.J., Van Nostrand, 1962. For a good critique of these, see also P. R. Breggin, "Psychotherapy as Applied Ethics," *Psychiatry*, Vol. 34 (Feb. 1971), pp. 59–74.

6 Halmos, *op. cit.*, pp. 105 and 104, respectively; see pp. 90–105.

7 T. Szasz, *The Ethics of Psychoanalysis. The Theory and Method of Autonomous Psychotherapy*, N.Y., Basic Books, 1965.

8 Halleck, for example, recognizes that therapy is political but does not adequately analyze the political assumptions entailed in "autonomous" psychotherapy. See Halleck, *op. cit.*

9 John McKnight, "Professionalized Service and Disabling Help," in I. Illich, I. Zola, J. McKnight, J. Caplan and H. Shaiken, *Disabling Professions*, London, Marion Boyers, 1977, p. 85.

10 *Ibid.*, p. 78.

11 See D. Lee, "Are Basic Needs Ultimate?," *Freedom and Culture*, Englewood Cliffs, N.Y., Prentice-Hall, 1959, pp. 70–7. See also McKnight, *op. cit.*, pp. 69–91.

12 There is a large literature on this issue. One of the most prominent critics of mental and social malfunctions as biologically-based is T. Szasz, *The Myth of Mental Illness; Foundations of a Theory of Personal Conduct*, N.Y., Hoeber-Harper, 1961. For a partial bibliography, see R. B. Edwards, *Psychiatry and Ethics, Insanity, Rational Autonomy, and Mental Health Care*, Buffalo, N.Y., Prometheus, 1982, pp. 139–42. See also, M. Edelman, "The Political Language of the Helping Professional," in *Things That Matter. Influences on Helping Relationships*, ed by H. Rubenstein and M. Bloch, N.Y., Macmillan, 1982, pp. 63–76.

13 Breggin brings out this point in Breggin, *op. cit.* He makes this critique of E. Erikson and F. Alexander.

14 Engelhardt, Jr, *op. cit.*, p. 444.

15 F. E. McDermott (ed.), *Self-Determination in Social Work, A Collection of Essays on Self-Determination and Related Concepts by Philosophers and Social Work Theorists*, Boston, Routledge & Kegan Paul, 1975.

16 These differences are described in R. Dana, *Human Services for Cultural Minorities*, Baltimore, University Park Press, 1981, Section III, pp. 185–282.

17 An adequate, short definition of racism is probably impossible, because racism differs significantly in its individual and institutional forms and in its covert, attitudinal and behavioral forms. To borrow part of Billingsley and Giovannoni's definition, it is "the systematic oppression, subjugation and control of one racial group, by another dominant or more powerful racial group, made possible by the manner in which the society is structured." A. Billingsley and J. Giovannoni, *Children of the Storm, Black Children and American Child Welfare*, N.Y., Harcourt Brace Jovanovich, 1972, p. 8. Some of the concepts in this definition would need elaboration in a full, theoretical account, but for the purposes of this chapter a working definition of racism is attitudes or behavior which express the inferiority or oppression of non-Caucasian racial groups. Racism will vary in its expression and in its centrality to a person's belief system, and one cannot always tell when it is present. For example, in discussions of reverse discrimination, or in a client's critical comments about a Black co-worker, a therapist may be uncertain whether or not the client is expressing racist attitudes. In addition, clients and workers may have racist attitudes which they are careful not to express.

18 *Code of Ethics of the National Association of Social Workers*, Washington, D.C., N.A.S.W., 1980, II F3, IV L3, VI.

19 C. Joffe, "What Abortion Counselors Want From Their Clients," *Social Problems* (Oct. 1978), pp. 112–21.

20 *Ibid.*, p. 114.

21 *Ibid.*

22 *Ibid.*

23 "Crisis Pregnancy Centers: An Alternative to Abortion," *Sharing*, Project Share, Vol. 8, No. 2 (July/Aug. 1984), p. 3; this was a summary of an article by Martin Mawyer in *Moody Monthly*, (Dec. 1982).
(Dec. 1982).

24 Even Chicana counselors are apt to have a significantly different value system from hers, because of their professional training.

25 For documentation of this outlook, see Dana, *op. cit.*, Section III; see also C. Medina and M. Reyes, "Dilemmas of Chicana Counselors," in *Things That Matter, Influences on Helping Relationships*, ed by H. Rubenstein and M. Bloch, N.Y., Macmillan, 1982, pp. 338–43.

26 M. K. Ho, "Social Work with Asian Americans," in R. H. Dana, *op. cit.*, p. 311; see all of Section IV on Asian Americans.

27 P. R. Breggin, "Psychiatry and Psychotherapy as Political Processes," *American Journal of Psychotherapy* (July 1975), Vol. 29, No. 3, p. 381.

28 *Ibid.*

29 See, for example, J. Kovel, *The Age of Desire. Reflections of a Radical Psychoanalyst*, N.Y., Pantheon, 1981; and J. Galper, *Social Work Practice, A Radical Perspective*, Engelwood Cliffs, N.J., Prentice-Hall, 1980.
30 Breggin, "Psychiatry and Psychotherapy as Political Processes," *op. cit.*, p. 379.
31 G. G. Jackson, "The Emergence of a Black Perspective in Counseling," in Dana, *op. cit.*, p. 131.
32 See, for example, Halmos, *op. cit.*
33 See APA, *Diagnostic and Statistical Manual of Mental Disorders (DSM III)*, Washington, D.C., American Psychiatric Association, 1980.
34 J. Margolis, "The Concept of a Disease," *Journal of Medicine and Philosophy*, 1976, Vol. 1, No. 3, pp. 238–55.
35 See *DSM III, op. cit.*, p. 6.
36 *Ibid.*
37 *Code of Ethics of the National Association of Social Workers, op. cit.*, II. F.3, IV L.3, VI.
38 Much has been written on this topic. See, for example, A. Thomas and S. Sillen, *Racism and Psychiatry*, N.Y., Brunner/Mazel, 1972.
39 Breggin, "Psychotherapy as Applied Ethics," *op. cit.*, p. 69.
40 McDermott, *op. cit.*
41 Breggin, "Psychotherapy as Applied Ethics," *op. cit.*, p. 61.
42 "Liberal" is admittedly imprecise, covering a range of utilitarian and rights' perspectives. See Chapter 2.
43 See A. Bry, *EST. 60 Hours That Transform Your Life*, N.Y., Avon, 1976.
44 McKnight, *op. cit.*, pp. 86, 87.

5 Directing the client: when is coercion justified?

1 I. Berlin, *Two Concepts of Liberty*, Oxford, Clarendon Press, 1958, p. 17.
2 L. Trilling, "Manners, Morals and the Novel," taken from D. Rothman, "The State as Parent: Social Policy in the Progressive Era," in W. Baylin *et al.*, *Doing Good. The Limits of Benevolence*, N.Y., Pantheon, 1978, p. 72.
3 This is meant as a working definition, whose terms and ambiguities will be made clearer by subsequent analysis.
4 Fotion defines paternalism in these terms; see N. Fotion, "Paternalism," *Ethics*, 89, 1979, pp. 191–8.
5 For an analysis of some of these definitions, see C. M. Culver and B. Gert, "Paternalistic Behavior," in *Philosophy and Medicine. Conceptual and Ethical Issues in Medicine and Psychiatry*, N.Y., Oxford University, 1982, pp. 126–42. A related issue is that of how much discretion a social worker should have in making decisions about others' lives. See, for example, M. Adler and S. Asquith (eds), *Discretion and Welfare*, London, Heinemann Educational Books, 1981.

6 This usage is brought out in Culver and Gert, *op. cit.*
7 H. Fingarette, *On Responsibility*, N.Y., Basic Books, 1967, pp. 155, 156.
8 Some of these questions are taken from the analysis by Culver and Gert, *op. cit.*, pp. 143–63.
9 For an interesting discussion of the issue of competence, see R. Macklin, "Refusal of Psychiatric Treatment: Autonomy, Competence and Paternalism," in R. B. Edwards (ed.), *Psychiatry and Ethics*, Buffalo, Prometheus, 1982, pp. 331–40. See also, G. Bermant, H. Kelman and D. Warwick (eds), *The Ethics of Social Intervention*, N.Y., John Wiley, 1978, Ch. 18; and L. Roth, A. Meisel and C. Lidz, "Tests of Competency to Consent to Treatment," *American Journal of Psychiatry*, 134 (1977), pp. 279–84.
10 It is sometimes argued that "authority," defined as "legitimate power," is a more appropriate term. Since, however, one of the issues is whether this sort of power is legitimate, I prefer the term "power."
11 Clients' descriptions, fictional and real, of this sort of coercion are particularly compelling in dramatizing the unfairness of these actions. See, for example, "The Woman Who had Five Husbands," and other stories in N. Tyre, *Red Wine First*, N.Y., Simon & Schuster, 1947; or B. Emecheta, *In The Ditch*, London, Alison & Busby, 1979.
12 For one example of this, see Culver and Gert, *op. cit.*
13 While coercion of this sort requires legal action, the legal resources of a poor, Black client do not compare to those of white, middle-class clients.
14 See again, Bermant *et al.*, *op. cit.* Ruth Macklin's discussion of competence and power is also useful (note 9). See also the bibliography of suggested reading in R. B. Edwards, *op. cit.*, pp. 341–4.
15 For further discussion of definitions of "manipulation," see N. Timms, *Social Work Values: An Enquiry*, London, Routledge & Kegan Paul, 1983, pp. 61–3; see also, A. Ware, "The Concept of Manipulation: Its Relation to Democracy and Power," *British Journal of Political Science*, 11, 2, (April 1981), pp. 163–81.
16 C. Whittington, "Self-Determination Re-examined," in F. E. McDermott (ed.), *Self-Determination in Social Work. A Collection of Essays on Self-Determination and Related Concepts by Philosophers and Social Work Theorists*, Boston, Routledge & Kegan Paul, 1975, p. 90.
17 See, for example, M. Greenspan, *A New Approach to Women and Therapy*, N.Y., McGraw-Hill, 1983.
18 See E. Mayer and N. Timms, *The Client Speaks. Working Class Impressions of Casework*, N.Y., Atherton, 1970. See also, A. Jones and A. A. Seagull, "Dimensions of the Relationship between the Black Client and the White Therapist. A Theoretical Overview," in R. Dana, *Human Services for Cultural Minorities*, Baltimore, University Park Press, 1981, pp. 150, 151; and see E. Mizio,

"White Worker-Minority Client" and M. S. Griffith, "The Influences of Race on the Psychotherapeutic Relationship," in H. Rubenstein and M. Bloch, *Things That Matter. Influences on Helping Relationships*, N.Y., Macmillan, 1982, pp. 191–5, 196–210, respectively.

19 This argument is made by Bermant *et al.*, *op. cit.*

20 This description of transference is of necessity oversimplified. The literature is vast and growing; for discussion of the issue, see, for example, G. H. Pollock and J. E. Gedo (eds), *Psychoanalysis: The Vital Issues, Vol. 2, Clinical Psychoanalysis and its Applications*, N.Y., International University Press, 1984.

21 "Feminism" can be defined in different ways. Assume that the social worker's feminism includes the beliefs that women are oppressed in our society and that action should be taken to create equality of opportunity and equal treatment for women. In addition, in Greenspan's words, "The ultimate goal of a genuinely feminist therapy must be to help a woman see how her own power as an individual is inextricably bound to the collective power of women as a group," Greenspan, *op. cit.*, p. 142.

22 C. Joffe, "What Abortion Counselors Want From Their Clients," *Social Problems* (Oct. 1978), pp. 112–21.

23 *Ibid.*

24 "Police Cadet talks Man out of Suicide," *Boston Globe*, 28 Nov. 1982.

25 For a good discussion of the ethics of lying, see S. Bok, *Lying*, N.Y., Vintage, 1979.

26 T. Szasz, *The Ethics of Psychoanalysis*, N.Y., Basic Books, 1965.

27 This point is mentioned by R. Macklin in "Refusal of Psychiatric Treatment: Autonomy, Competence, and Paternalism," *op. cit.*, p. 338.

28 Clients' perplexity is beautifully illustrated in Mayer and Timms, *op. cit.*

6 Dealing with bureacracy

1 H. H. Perlman, "Social Casework in Social Work," *Casework Within Social Work*, ed G. Parker, University of Newcastle Press, 1973, p. 9, cited by G. Pearson, *The Deviant Imagination. Psychiatry, Social Work and Social Change*, N.Y., Holmes & Meier, 1975, pp. 135, 136.

2 G. Konrad, *The Case Worker*, trans. by P. Aston, N.Y., Harcourt Brace Jovanovich, 1974, p. 11.

3 Three million of the 4.3 million "service professionals" are in the public sector. See D. Johnson and C. O'Donnell, "The Accumulation Crisis and Service Professionals," in K. Fox *et al. Crisis in the Public Sector. A Reader*, N.Y., Monthly Review Press, 1982, p. 34; taken from A. Withorn, *Serving the People. Social Services and Social Change*, N.Y., Columbia University, 1984, p. 159.

4 For a particularly good account of this, see M. Lipsky, *Street-Level*

Bureaucracy, Dilemmas of the Individual in Public Services, N.Y., Russell Sage Foundation, 1980.

5 See, for example, Harold L. Wilensky and Charles N. Lebeaux, *Industrial Society and Social Welfare*, N.Y., Russell Sage Foundation, 1958; Charles Schottland (ed.), *The Welfare State*, N.Y., Harper & Row, 1967.

6 M. Weber, *Max Weber on Capitalism, Bureaucracy, and Religion: A Selection of Texts*, ed and trans. by S. Andreski, Boston, Allen & Unwin, 1983.

7 See, for example, Charles Perrow, *Complex Organizations*, Chicago, Scott Foresman, 1971, or A. Etzioni (ed.), *Complex Organizations: A Sociological Reader*, N.Y., Holt, Rinehart & Winston, 1961. Y. Hasenfeld and R. A. English, *Human Service Organizations. A Book of Readings*, Ann Arbor, University of Michigan, 1974.

8 In my analysis, I draw particularly on John Ladd's critique of bureaucracies and on conversations with Ann Withorn. See J. Ladd, "Morality and the Ideal of Rationality in Formal Organizations," *Monist* (October 1970), Vol. 54, 4; "Is 'Corporate Responsibility' a Coherent Notion?" in *Proceedings of the Second National Conference on Business Ethics*, ed by M. Hoffman, Washington, D.C., University Press of America, 1979, pp. 102–13.

9 Ladd, "Is 'Corporate Responsibility' a Coherent Notion?," *op. cit.*, p. 105.

10 See, for example, Ladd, "Morality and the Ideal of Rationality in Formal Organizations," *op. cit.*; or E. Litwik, "Models of Bureaucracy Which Permit Conflict," in Y. Hasenfeld and R. A. English, *op. cit.*, pp. 417–28.

11 K. E. Goodpaster and J. B. Matthews, Jr, "Can a Corporation Have a Conscience?," *Harvard Business Review* (Jan.-Feb. 1982), p. 134.

12 Lipsky, *op. cit.*, p. 72.

13 R. M. Emerson and M. Pollner, "Dirty-Work Designations: Their Features and Consequences in a Psychiatric Setting," in H. Rubenstein and M. H. Bloch, *Things That Matter. Influences on Helping Relationships*, N.Y., Macmillan, 1982, p. 382. See also, E. Hughes, "Good People and Dirty Work," in *The Sociological Eye. Selected Papers*, Chicago, Aldine Atherton, 1971, pp. 87–97.

14 Ladd, "Morality and the Ideal of Rationality in Formal Organizations," *op. cit.*, p. 511.

15 J. Prottas, *People-Processing: The Street Level Bureaucrat in Public Service Bureaucracies*, Lexington, Mass., Lexington Books, 1979, p. 169.

16 There is a large literature on this. See, for example, M. Adler and S. Asquith, *Discretion and Welfare*, London, Heinemann, 1981; Hasenfeld and English, *op. cit.*, A. Withorn, *op. cit.*

17 G. Smith, "Discretionary Decision-Making in Social Work," Adler

and Asquith, *op. cit.*, p. 54.
18 Lipsky, *op. cit.*, p. 59.
19 See Lipsky, *op. cit.*, p. 14; see also G. Smith, *op. cit.*
20 See, for example, A. Withorn, *The Circle Game. Services for the Poor in Massachusetts, 1966–1978*, Amherst, University of Massachusetts, 1982 or Milwaukee County Welfare Rights Organization, *Welfare Mothers Speak Out: we ain't gonna shuffle anymore*, ed by T. H. Tarantino and D. Becker, N.Y., Norton, 1972.
21 See Lipsky, *op. cit.*
22 Withorn, *The Circle Game*, *op. cit.*, p. 80.
23 See *ibid.*, pp. 78, 79.
24 T. Prosser, "The Politics of Discretion: Aspects of Discretionary Power in the Supplementary Benefits Scheme," in Adler and Asquith, *op. cit.*, p. 150.
25 For discussion of sexual misconduct in therapeutic relationships, see, for example, V. Davidson, "Psychiatry's Problem with No Name: Therapist-Patient Sex," in E. Howell and M. Bayes (eds), *Women and Mental Health*, N.Y., Basic Books, 1981, pp. 141–9.
26 For one excellent discussion of this aspect of bureaucracies in Nazi Germany, see H. Arendt, *Eichmann in Jerusalem: A Report on the Banality of Evil*, N.Y., Viking, 1963.
27 Interview with a human service worker.
28 For further discussion of this, see J. Galper, *Social Work Practice, A Radical Perspective*, N.J., Prentice-Hall, 1980; Daphne Stratham, *Radicals in Social Work*, London, Routledge & Kegan Paul, 1978; Withorn, *Serving the People*, *op. cit.*
29 For more on unions in social work, see, E. Phillipson Cole, "Unions in Social Work," *NASW Encyclopedia of Social Work*, 16 (1973), pp. 1507–11; Milton Tambor, "The Social Worker as Worker: A Union Perspective," *Administration in Social Work*, 3 (3), 1979, pp. 289–300.
30 Self-termed radical social workers discuss this. See note 28.
31 Withorn, *The Circle Game*, *op. cit.*, p. 18.
32 See, for example, M. Mahaffey and J. Hanks (eds), *Practical Politics. Social Work and Political Responsibility*, Maryland, N.A.S.W. 1982.
33 One example of this is the success of some workers in Massachusetts in forming an alliance with clients to change regulations harmful to clients. Linda Stacey, panelist on workshop, "Client-Worker Relations: Women against Women?," Women and Poverty Conference, University of Massachusetts/Boston, 14 April 1984.
34 Withorn, *The Circle Game*, *op. cit.*, pp. 16 and 149, respectively.

7 Creating empathy and doing good

1 George Konrad, *The Case Worker*, trans. by P. Aston, N.Y., Harcourt Brace Jovanovich, 1974, p. 14.
2 Roy Lubove, *The Professional Altruist. The Emergence of Social*

Work As a Career, 1880–1930, Cambridge, Mass., Harvard University Press, 1965, pp. 15, 16.

3 Simone Weil, *The Simone Weil Reader*, ed by G. A. Panichas, N.Y., David McKay, 1977, p. 371.

4 I do not mean to gloss over significant differences in worker-client relationships, depending on the nature of the service, agency, resources, etc. Despite these differences, this sort of relationship is posited as the ideal. See standard social work textbooks, such as H. H. Perlman, *Relationship, The Heart of Helping People*, Chicago, University of Chicago, 1979.

5 S. Rees, *Social Work Face to Face*, N.Y., Columbia, 1979, p. 54.

6 *Ibid.*

7 H. H. Perlman, *op. cit.*, p. 54. My italics.

8 Paul Halmos, *The Faith of the Counsellors. A Study in the Theory and Practices of Social Case Work and Psychotherapy*, N.Y., Schocken, 1970, pp. 105, 104, respectively.

9 Rees, *op. cit.*, p. 99.

10 E. Sainsbury, *Social Work with Families. Perceptions of Social Casework among Clients of a Family Service Unit*, London, Routledge & Kegan Paul, 1974, p. 50.

11 John E. Mayer and N. Timms, *The Client Speaks. Working Class Impressions of Casework*, N.Y., Atherton, 1970, p. 116.

12 Sainsbury, *op. cit.*, p. 87.

13 Ann Withorn, *Serving the People. Social Services and Social Change*, N.Y., Columbia University, 1984, p. 122.

14 Rees, *op. cit.*, p. 47.

15 *Ibid.*, p. 51.

16 Ann Withorn, *The Circle Game. Services for the Poor in Massachussets, 1966–1978*, Amherst, University of Massachussets, 1982, p. 128.

17 *Ibid.*, p. 139.

18 G. Pearson, *The Deviant Imagination. Psychiatry, Social Work and Social Change*, N.Y., Holmes & Meier, 1975, p. 133.

19 Rees *op. cit.*, p. 95.

20 Sainsbury, *op. cit.*, p. 86.

21 *Ibid.*, p. 89.

22 This was true for all three of the studies cited – Mayer and Timms, Rees, and Sainsbury. See also, for example, T. Keefe and D. E. Maypole, *Relationships in Social Service Practice. Context and Skills*, Monterey, Calif., Wadsworth, 1983, p. 62.

23 Sainsbury, *op. cit.*, p. 52.

24 *Ibid.*, Chs 6 and 9.

25 See, for example, R. H. Dana (ed.), *Human Services for Cultural Minorities*, Baltimore, University Park Press, 1981.

26 "Professional relationship" is loosely defined as one which is "limited by requirements of treatment or social role," Sainsbury, *op. cit.*, p. 71.

27 *Ibid.*, p. 105.

28 *Ibid.*, p. 105.
29 Withorn, *The Circle Game*, *op. cit.*, p. 139.
30 M. North, *The Secular Priests*, London, Allen & Unwin, 1972, pp. 291, 292, quoted in Pearson, *op. cit.*, p. 138.
31 Keefe and Maypole, *op. cit.*, p. 66.
32 *Ibid.*
33 Mayer and Timms, *op. cit.*, p. 114.
34 Sainsbury, *op. cit.*, p. 33.
35 Mayer and Timms, *op. cit.*, p. 114, taken from E. E. Irvine, "The Hard-To-Like Family," *Case Conference*, Vol. 14 (July 1967), p. 108.
36 Ira Glasser, "Prisoners of Benevolence: Power versus Liberty in the Welfare State," in Willard Gaylin, I. Glasser, S. Marcus and D. Rothman, *Doing Good. The Limits of Benevolence*, N.Y., Pantheon, 1978, p. 165.
37 *Ibid.*, p. 117.
38 *Ibid.*, pp. 123, 124.
39 R. Plant, H. Lesser, P. Taylor, *Political Philosophy and Social Welfare: Essays on the Normative Basis of Welfare Provision*, London, Routledge & Kegan Paul, 1980, p. 53.
40 Richard Titmuss, *The Gift Relationship, From Human Blood to Social Policy*, N.Y., Pantheon, 1971.
41 Sainsbury, *op. cit.*, p. 33.
42 One of my colleagues attributed this quotation to C. Chavez, from H. Anderson, *So Shall Ye Reap*, N.Y., Crowell, 1970, but I have been unable to locate the quotation in that book.
43 Withorn, *The Circle Game*, *op. cit.*, p. 89.
44 Mayer and Timms, *op. cit.*, p. 77.
45 Withorn, *The Circle Game*, *op. cit.*, p. 15.

Further reading

The following list consists of works which I have found to be particularly useful to students unfamiliar with philosophy. It is not intended to be complete but rather offers some suggestions for beginning study of ethical issues in human services.

For a useful and less idiosyncratic list, see "Ethical Issues in the Human Services, Syllabi and Bibliography," ed by A. Preus, Director, National Endowment for the Humanities, Division of Education Programs, 1982.

General works

H. Arendt, *Eichmann in Jerusalem, A Report on the Banality of Evil*, N.Y., Penguin, 1963.

L. Blum, *Friendship, Altruism, and Morality*, Boston, Routledge & Kegan Paul, 1980.

D. Callahan and H. T. Engelhardt, Jr, *The Roots of Ethics, Science, Religion and Values*, N.Y., Plenum, 1976.

J. Feinberg, *Social Philosophy*, Englewood Cliffs, N.J., Prentice-Hall, 1973.

J. Feinberg, *Rights, Justice and the Bounds of Liberty: Essays in Social Philosophy*, Englewood Cliffs, N.J., Prentice-Hall, 1980.

H. Fingarette, *On Responsibility*, N.Y., Basic Books, 1967.

W. K. Frankena, *Ethics*, Englewood Cliffs, N.J., Prentice-Hall, 1973.

W. K. Frankena, *Thinking About Ethics*, Ann Arbor, University of Michigan, 1980.

A. Jagger, *Feminist Politics and Human Nature*, N.J., Rowman & Allenheld, 1983.

J. Ladd, "Morality and the Ideal of Rationality in Formal Organizations," *Monist*, Vol. 54, No. 4, (October 1970).

J. Ladd, "Legalism and Medical Ethics," in *Biomedical Ethics*, ed John W. Davis, Hoffmeister & Shorten, Humana Press, 1978.

A. MacIntyre, *A Short History of Ethics*, N.Y., Macmillan, 1966.

A. MacIntyre, *After Virtue, A Study in Moral Theory*, Indiana, Notre Dame Press, 1981.

J.S. Mill, *On Liberty*, ed by E. Rapaport, Indianapolis, Hackett, 1978.

I. Murdoch, *The Sovereignty of Good*, N.Y., Schocken, 1971.

J. Rawls, *A Theory of Justice*, Cambridge, Mass., Belknap, 1971.

P. Singer, *Practical Ethics*, Cambridge, Cambridge University, 1979.

J. C. Smart and B. Williams, *Utilitarianism: For and Against*, Cambridge, Cambridge University, 1973.

B. Williams, *Morality: An Introduction to Ethics*, N.Y., Harper & Row, 1972.

Social work ethics

R. Bailey and M. Brake (eds), *Radical Social Work*, N.Y., Pantheon, 1975.
G. Bermant *et al.* (eds), *The Ethics of Social Intervention*, N.Y., John Wiley, 1978.
S. Bok, *Lying. Moral Choice in Public and Private Life*, N.Y., Vintage, 1979.
S. Bok, *Secrets, On the Ethics of Concealment and Revelation*, N.Y., Pantheon, 1982.
C. Culver and B. Gert, *Philosophy in Medicine*, N.Y., Oxford University, 1982.
R. S. Downie and E. Telfer, *Caring and Curing. A Philosophy of Medicine and Social Work*, N.Y., Methuen, 1980.
W. Gaylin *et al.*, *Doing Good. The Limits of Benevolence*, N.Y., Pantheon, 1978.
I. Illich *et al.*, *Disabling Professions*, London, Marion Boyers, 1977.
C. S. Levy, *Social Work Ethics*, N.Y., Human Sciences, 1976.
F. E. McDermott (ed.), *Self-Determination in Social Work, A Collection of Essays on Self-Determination and Related Concepts by Philosophers and Social Work Theorists*, Boston, Routledge & Kegan Paul, 1975.
R. Plant, *Social and Moral Theory in Casework*, London, Routledge & Kegan Paul, 1970.
R. Plant, H. Lesser and P. Taylor, *Political Philosophy and Social Welfare: Essays on the Normative Basis of Welfare Provision*, London, Routledge & Kegan Paul, 1980.
F. G. Reamer, *Ethical Dilemmas in Social Service*, N.Y., Columbia, 1982.
H. Rubenstein and M. Bloch (eds), *Things That Matter, Influences on Helping Relationships*, N.Y., Macmillan, 1982.
N. Timms, *Social Welfare: Why and How?*, Boston, Routledge & Kegan Paul, 1980.
N. Timms, *Social Work Values: An Enquiry*, Boston, Routledge & Kegan Paul, 1983.
N. Timms and D. Watson (eds), *Philosophy in Social Work*, Boston, Routledge & Kegan Paul, 1978.
R. Titmuss, *The Gift Relationship, From Human Blood to Social Policy*, N.Y., Pantheon, 1971.
S. Wilson, *Confidentiality in Social Work*, N.Y., Free Press, 1978.
E. Younghusband, *Social Work and Social Values*, London, Allen & Unwin, 1967.